ROUTLEDGE LIBRARY EDITIONS:
LIBRARY AND INFORMATION SCIENCE

Volume 78

THE ROLE OF CONFERENCE LITERATURE IN SCI-TECH LIBRARIES

THE ROLE OF CONFERENCE LITERATURE IN SCI-TECH LIBRARIES

Edited by
ELLIS MOUNT

Taylor & Francis Group

LONDON AND NEW YORK

First published in 1989 by The Haworth Press, Inc.

This edition first published in 2020
by Routledge
2 Park Square, Milton Park, Abingdon, Oxon OX14 4RN

and by Routledge
52 Vanderbilt Avenue, New York, NY 10017

Routledge is an imprint of the Taylor & Francis Group, an informa business

© 1989 The Haworth Press, Inc.

All rights reserved. No part of this book may be reprinted or reproduced or utilised in any form or by any electronic, mechanical, or other means, now known or hereafter invented, including photocopying and recording, or in any information storage or retrieval system, without permission in writing from the publishers.

Trademark notice: Product or corporate names may be trademarks or registered trademarks, and are used only for identification and explanation without intent to infringe.

British Library Cataloguing in Publication Data
A catalogue record for this book is available from the British Library

ISBN: 978-0-367-34616-4 (Set)
ISBN: 978-0-429-34352-0 (Set) (ebk)
ISBN: 978-0-367-36450-2 (Volume 78) (hbk)
ISBN: 978-0-367-36451-9 (Volume 78) (pbk)
ISBN: 978-0-429-34618-7 (Volume 78) (ebk)

Publisher's Note
The publisher has gone to great lengths to ensure the quality of this reprint but points out that some imperfections in the original copies may be apparent.

Disclaimer
The publisher has made every effort to trace copyright holders and would welcome correspondence from those they have been unable to trace.

The Role of Conference Literature in Sci-Tech Libraries

Ellis Mount
Editor

The Haworth Press
New York • London

The Role of Conference Literature in Sci-Tech Libraries has also been published as *Science & Technology Libraries*, Volume 9, Number 2, Winter 1988.

© 1989 by The Haworth Press, Inc. All rights reserved. No part of this book may be reproduced or utilized in any form or by any means, electronic or mechanical, including photocopying, microfilm and recording, or by any information storage and retrieval system, without permission in writing from the publisher. Printed in the United States of America.

The Haworth Press, Inc., 10 Alice Street, Binghamton, NY 13904-1580
EUROSPAN/Haworth, 3 Henrietta Street, London WC2E 8LU England

Library of Congress Cataloging-in-Publication Data

The Role of conference literature in sci-tech libraries / Ellis Mount, editor.
    p. cm.
    "Has also been published as Science & technology libraries, volume 9, number 2, winter 1988"—T.p. verso.
    Includes bibliographies.
    ISBN 0-86656-780-1
    1. Libraries—Special collections—Conference proceedings. 2. Scientific libraries—Collection development. 3. Technical libraries—Collection development. 4. Conference proceedings—Bibliography—Methodology. I. Mount, Ellis.
Z688.L667R64   1989
026'.5—dc19   86-1705
                                                            CIP

The Role of Conference Literature in Sci-Tech Libraries

CONTENTS

Introduction	xi
Living with Conference Proceedings: An Analysis of the Problems, Pitfalls, and Successful Techniques for Access	1
Loren D. Mendelsohn	
James A. Ruffner	
Primary Sources and Primary Confusion	3
Problems of User Education	4
Techniques for Locating Conference Proceedings	5
Indexes Useful for Obtaining or Verifying Full Bibliographic Information	7
On Leaving Some Stones Unturned	9
Searching Procedures (For Library Catalogs)	11
Examples	13
Conclusion	17
Publishing of Sci-Tech Conference Proceedings: Viewpoint of an Editor	21
James L. Smith	
Production Schedules	21
Market Outlook	23
Review Type Publications	25
Future Outlook	27
Cataloging Conference Publications: Problems and Issues	29
Michael S. Borries	
Serials or Monographs	29
Title and Name Changes	30
Cataloging Rules	31

Coverage of Conference Documents in Scientific Databases: Viewpoint of Cambridge Scientific Abstracts   35
    Jonathan R. L. Sears

Introduction   35
Accessing Conference Documents   37
Conclusion   44

Secondary Publisher Coverage of Engineering Conference Papers: Viewpoint of Engineering Information, Inc.   47
    Gloria Moline

Introduction   47
Characteristics of the Engineering Conference Literature Covered by Ei   48
Identifying, Selecting and Ordering Conference Proceedings   53
Current and Future Challenges   60

InterDok Corporation Publications for the Identification and Acquisition of the Sci-Tech Conference Proceedings Literature   63
    Bernard B. Baschkin
    Karen-Anne Baschkin

Sources of Information   63
Editorial Processes   65
InterDok Publications   65
Supporting Services   67
A Look Ahead   70

Conference Proceedings at the Engineering Societies Library   73
    Kirk Cabeen

Role of Conference Literature   73
Procedures at ESL   74

Conference Proceedings: A Tutorial Module   77
    Nestor L. Osorio

Introduction   77
Bibliographic Description   80

Methodology	86
Results	89

SCI-TECH COLLECTIONS — 95
Tony Stankus, Editor

Supernovae: A Guide to the Literature — 97
David Stern

What Is a Supernova?	97
Recent Activity	98
Importance of the New Observations	99
Impact on the Literature	100
Finding the Available Resources	100
Popular Material	101
Research Material	104

NEW REFERENCE WORKS IN SCIENCE AND TECHNOLOGY — 119
Arleen N. Somerville, Editor

SCI-TECH IN REVIEW — 133
Karla Pearce, Editor
Giuliana Lavendel, Associate Editor

SCI-TECH ONLINE — 141
Ellen Nagle, Editor

Ninth National Online Meeting	141
Database News	142
Search System News	144
Publications and Search Aids	145

Introduction

Most librarians working with sci-tech collections are fully aware of the importance of conference papers and proceedings. Quite often the first public disclosure of important sci-tech developments or discoveries occurs at conferences, symposia, or meetings having similar designations. At the same time the problems of dealing with conference literature are also well known to sci-tech librarians, including difficulties of cataloging, identifying, selecting and obtaining pieces of conference literature. Still another development is that of online access to conference literature, as well as through printed reference tools.

The aim of this issue is to present a variety of viewpoints on conference literature, including that of librarians, commercial publishers, producers of indexing/abstracting tools, catalogers and editors.

The first paper discusses the viewpoints of two sci-tech librarians, Loren D. Mendelsohn and James A. Ruffner at Wayne State University, on the problems of accessing, citing and locating conference literature. In the next paper James L. Smith, an editor at John Wiley & Sons, Inc., describes the difficulties in editing a set of conference papers in book form. Many aspects of the cataloging of conference publications are described by Michael S. Borries, a serials cataloger at Columbia University Libraries.

The next three papers present the viewpoints of publishers who provide indexing/abstracting services as well as a certain amount of document delivery for conference literature. The first of the three is by Jonathan R. L. Sears of Cambridge Scientific Abstracts. Next is the paper by Gloria Moline, of Engineering Information, Inc. The last is by Bernard B. Baschkin and Karen-Anne Baschkin. These three papers describe their selection methods, retrieval services and general outlook on conference literature.

The next paper discusses the types of conference literature col-

© 1989 by The Haworth Press, Inc. All rights reserved.

lected at the Engineering Societies Library, written by Kirk Cabeen, who also covers their cataloging and lending procedures. The last paper, by Nestor L. Osorio, of Northern Illinois University, presents a tutorial module for instructing students in the use of conference proceedings.

The collection development paper for this issue is written by David Stern at the University of Illinois. His topic is Supernovae, one of the major areas of current interest among astronomers.

Along with the Sci-Tech in Review and Sci-Tech Online sections, prepared by their regular editors, this issue includes the first section (New Reference Works in Science and Technology) edited by Arleen N. Somerville, who is Head of Science and Engineering Libraries, University of Rochester. She is replacing Robert Krupp, who had to resign from this post due to health reasons. We owe him a vote of thanks for the many excellent issues of this section which he edited.

Ellis Mount
Editor

Living with Conference Proceedings: An Analysis of the Problems, Pitfalls, and Successful Techniques for Access

Loren D. Mendelsohn
James A. Ruffner

SUMMARY. Conference literature forms a vital communication link in many fields of science and engineering. The problems of accessing this literature are analyzed in terms of typical citation and cataloging practices. Problems of user education and location techniques are outlined, recommended search practices and common pitfalls are indicated, and examples are provided.

Conference proceedings represent one of the most difficult aspects of library work from any point of view: acquisition, budget constraints, cataloging, bibliographic instruction, reference, or access.[1-6] On any given day of the year a thousand or more papers are being read at conferences, workshops, or other meetings. Some or all of the papers from a given meeting may be collected and published as books, special journal issues, government documents, reports or elsewhere in the "gray" literature. Other papers are available only as separate preprints. Major societies may be responsible

---

Loren D. Mendelsohn is Assistant Director, Science and Engineering Library, Wayne State University, Detroit, MI 48202. He holds a BS in Biochemistry from the State University of New York at Binghamton, the MS in Biological Chemistry and the MA in Library Science both from the University of Michigan. James A. Ruffner is Academic Service Officer, Science and Engineering Library, Wayne State University. He holds the BSc in Physics from the Ohio State University, the MS in Meteorology from the University of Michigan, and the AM and PhD in History and Philosophy of Science both from Indiana University.

© 1989 by The Haworth Press, Inc. All rights reserved.

for well over one hundred conference volumes per year, in addition to the proceedings of "independent" conferences. Publication may include the full text or a digested form, either of which may differ from the version actually delivered. Frequently, only abstracts are published. Even when no formal publication takes place, individual papers or sets may be distributed informally, drop into obscurity in personal files, only to surface again as references in other publications.

Questions are often raised about the quality and significance of conference literature on the grounds that *some* conference papers are never subjected to screening, selection, refereeing, or editing. Claims frequently are made that the good papers *usually* appear in the regular journal literature and that in any case the same material *may* be subject to repeated publication.[7-10] Even if these claims were true, they are irrelevant.[11]

Papers appearing in conference proceedings are not eligible for publication in many journals. While some authors "redigest" other readily available publications, most are unlikely to publish in ways that make the practice evident in their lists of publications. Since librarians have mainly bibliographic techniques at hand, they are unlikely to distinguish clearly between the rehasher and the author who provides something significantly different in each publication. It is presumptuous to attempt such distinctions unless one is extremely familiar with the literature of a particular subject. Singular devotion to an author's list of references is shortsighted, of course, because it trusts implicitly that person's bibliographic skills; however, librarians and beginning users, such as graduate students who generate most of the requests, should be wary of seeking substitutions too quickly.

The most common source of requests for conference papers is the citation an author makes to document a certain point. The user can have very good reasons for seeing the actual reference in its particular form. The extent to which other possible forms of that reference may be used is a very different matter, as discussed by Bates.[12] The user may be encouraged, indeed frequently should be encouraged, to seek other sources in addition to the desired item. Communication, particularly of methods or "know how," can be very difficult through the printed word. Only the user can decide after the item is in hand whether the reference has significance for his or her work.

PRIMARY SOURCES AND PRIMARY CONFUSION

Conference literature today is part of the heart and soul of engineering and computer science. To a large extent, it stands apart from the journal literature of the same subject, and is a primary form of publication. Additionally, in fast moving fields aided with rapid publication techniques frequently used for proceedings, conferences can be the sources of the latest detailed ideas or provocative suggestions as well as the best reviews or overviews of a topic. The quality may be variable, but generalizations about quality are hard to justify. Whatever may be true for some other fields, the advance of engineering and computer sciences depends significantly upon conference proceedings as a definitive form of communication, with volumes 10 or 15 years old sometimes sought as eagerly as the current ones. Current trends are away from very general, broad-based conferences toward an increasing multitude of highly focused specialty conferences.[13] Facilitating access to the full spectrum of conference literature is a prime responsibility of librarians.

Of significant importance to the matter of facilitating access is how conference proceedings are cataloged. Many conferences recur at intervals with their proceedings frequently published and cataloged as serials. Additionally, some organizations such as SPIE – The International Society for Optical Engineering publish conference series in which each volume is the proceedings of a differently named conference and therefore is usually cataloged monographically. When the proceedings of recurring conferences are cataloged as serials, access is limited to corporate authors and serial title (which will often differ from the name of the conference). When such conferences are cataloged monographically, names of editors, distinctive volume titles, and other available variable information are included.

Further complicating the matter is the fact that access to the conference literature through library catalogs or indexing and abstracting services often requires information significantly different from that provided in the lists of cited references.[14] Usually, these lists provide the most accurate information about the authors and titles of individual papers. In the case of citations to conference series, the reference will often include only the series title, volume, and page numbers. The completeness or accuracy concerning the title of the proceedings, the name of the conference, or the names of editors is subject to enormous variation, when such information is provided at all. The volume title will be absent in the majority of the citations, thus making it extremely difficult to locate the item using the online catalog or bibliographic utilities. These shortcomings may be due to the citing author or to the original editor and publisher.

At their best, matching citations with holdings records in one's own library or through bibliographic utilities such as OCLC or RLIN can be very difficult and time-consuming. Either librarians have to do most of the hard work themselves, or find ways to share a significant portion of that work by providing *simple* rules for matching citations with holdings records.

PROBLEMS OF USER EDUCATION

One problem for user education is distinguishing between the author of an individual paper and the editor of an overall volume, so that the proper name is searched in the catalog. This problem applies equally to journals and multiauthored books. Another problem is isolating a unique volume title, if any, from a complex proceedings entry, and distinguishing such a title from the title of the individual paper. The paper/volume title problem for conference citations typically is more difficult than that for journal and multiauthored book citations. The theory for instruction may be similar, but efficient practice may be more elusive.

The typical conference citation in a list of references includes the *name* of the conference cast either as a corporate author entry or with the addition of a rubric such as "proceedings of the . . ." as a title entry. The conceptual difficulty for most users involves seeing the conference name as an author and not as a title. The practical difficulty is the very large number of entries with nearly identical initial wording. Cataloging rules that dictate differences between serial and monographic entries, that depend on judgments as to degree of responsibility of the corporate body, and that differ by date of creation also present problems.[15] The general rule to drop information such as the number of a particular conference used as a corporate author in recurring series can be misapplied in title searching. The problems are particularly acute in online catalogs or in utilities such as OCLC and RLIN that use different protocols for author and title searching.

Acronyms present another problem of consistency. They may be a proper part of the corporate author or title entry derived from the title page and hence formally searchable in catalogs or indexes, or they may merely be informal shorthand known only to the author or insider group.

TECHNIQUES FOR LOCATING CONFERENCE PROCEEDINGS

The techniques of locating conference proceedings can be addressed on two levels: (1) techniques appropriate for librarians, and (2) techniques appropriate for users. Most of the resources in this area can be used effectively by users as well as librarians. The librarians' access to large bibliographic databases such as OCLC or RLIN, however, increases their options for access points.[16] Many of the printed and online indexes provide such information as LC card numbers, ISSNs, or ISBNs. Such items are relatively useless to the user while the librarian can usually use them to obtain accurate bibliographic information for specific proceedings volumes. Additionally, information in some indexes or in a bibliographic utility entry, such as the series tracings in fields 490, 440, or 830 of the MARC record, provide information on parallel publishing of a proceedings both as a special journal issue and as a monograph.

Users can be taught to use corporate authors as a search key, although it frequently falls to the librarian to accurately determine the searchable form of the corporate author name. This process can be relatively straightforward when the conference has been sponsored by a particular organization. Many conferences, however, are "independent" of any sponsoring organization. Moreover, the bibliographic information supplied in the list of citations at the end of a published paper frequently makes no reference to the sponsoring organization.

As mentioned previously, many organizations sponsor upwards of a hundred conferences annually. Thus, searching using the organization as the corporate author can be tedious at best. Fortunately, in many cases, the title of a conference can be used as a secondary corporate author. For example, the proceedings of the Robotic Intelligence and Productivity Conference, sponsored by Wayne State University, Department of Electrical and Computer Engineering, can be located using two corporate authors in both OCLC and the online catalog:

1. Wayne State University
2. Robotic Intelligence and Productivity Conference

The first of these entries generates more hits than OCLC can handle, requiring the tedious narrowing-down process. The second corporate author generates three hits on OCLC, a small enough number of records to be dealt with easily. This approach can be useful for the independent conferences as well as those sponsored by prolific organizations. Unfortunately, the user is left with the confusing situation of having to search some titles as authors and other apparently similar titles under a title key.

Searching can be performed on the title of a proceedings when available. Occasionally, the title of the conference doubles as the title of its proceedings. When this happens, the conference is usually independent, although sometimes this happens with conferences sponsored by organizations such as SPIE. Frequently, however, completely non-descriptive titles are given, restricted to words or phrases such as *Proceedings, Conference Record*, or *Abstracts and Papers*, making it extremely difficult to use the title as a search key. The problem is further complicated by the addition of the words "of the" in some cases, but not in others. Cataloging practices for titles vary so much that no one form of searching can be used. The best general advice is to avoid title searches if only generic non-descriptive titles are available.

INDEXES USEFUL FOR OBTAINING OR VERIFYING FULL BIBLIOGRAPHIC INFORMATION

The most comprehensive of all the various indexes available is probably the British Library Document Supply Centre's *Index of Conference Proceedings Received*. This center makes a significant effort to collect all conference proceedings. Their single index is arranged alphabetically by keywords in title, including names or acronyms of the sponsoring organizations. Under each keyword heading, the proceedings are arranged by conference date. Entries include the conference location and the ISBN or ISSN (Standard Numbers), if available. Titles of proceedings which are serially cataloged or which appear as special journal issues can be clarified by using the companion work, *Current Serials Received*. This index is computer searchable using the BLAISELINE system.

Another important index is the *Directory of Published Proceedings* published in various parts by the InterDok Corporation. It is less comprehensive than the *Index of Conference Proceedings Received*, and its indexing system is fairly difficult for most library patrons to use, but it contains comprehensive bibliographic information on proceedings volumes, including ISBN or ISSN and LC card number, if available. The indexes provide access by subject, sponsor, editor, and conference location. Additionally, the accession numbers begin with the month and year of the conference, providing limited access by date. It is interesting to note that the British Library Document Supply Centre and the InterDok Corporation rely on each other's publications to ensure the best possible coverage within their policies. [17-18]

A third index is *Proceedings in Print*, published by Proceedings in Print, Inc. It is the least comprehensive of the three. The bibliographic information provided is also less complete, lacking ISBN or ISSN and the LC card number. The primary advantage of this source is the fact that entries distinguish between the title of the conference and the title of the proceedings. Its single index covers editors and sponsors as well as subjects.

None of the three sources discussed above provides indexing at the level of individual papers, for which (as discussed above) the most accurate and complete information is usually provided. There are two general sources that, while less comprehensive, do provide indexing at the paper level.

The *Index to Scientific and Technical Proceedings* (ISTP), published by the Institute for Scientific Information, provides access by author and subject keyword in title. ISTP also indexes sponsoring organization, meeting locations, and corporate affiliations of the authors of individual papers. Entries include ISBN or ISSN and the LC card number. Also stated is the journal title, issue, and volume number of those proceedings which are special issues. Especially helpful are the complete tables of contents of every proceedings volume indexed.

Also useful is the *Conference Papers Index*, published by Cambridge Scientific Abstracts. The coverage is rather limited and the bibliographic information is of variable quality. This source is significant, however, because it provides addresses and information for ordering copies of the individual papers. The indexing (subject key word in title, author, topic of conference, and date of conference) provides very useful access points. This index is also computer searchable on the DIALOG system. It is important to understand that this index is oriented primarily toward the individual papers, not toward the proceedings volume.

Several specialized sources also provide indexing at the individual paper level. The Institution of Electrical Engineers produces, through its INSPEC division, the extremely powerful *Science Abstracts* now published in three sections, *Computer and Control Abstracts*, *Electrical and Electronics Abstracts*, and *Physics Abstracts*. These sources index journal articles and individual papers in select conference volumes as well as some monographs and other information sources, and are computer searchable through a variety of vendors. A bibliography of these conference proceedings included is provided in each semiannual index and cumulation. Many rare titles are included. ISBN or ISSN and LC card number are not provided.

The corresponding American society, the Institute of Electrical and Electronic Engineers, publishes only its own *Index to IEEE Publications*, which nonetheless deserves special mention given the enormous number of conferences sponsored annually by this organization. This source not only indexes individual papers, but also lists the names of all the conferences published by IEEE or its regional sections, together with complete bibliographic information on the proceedings volumes frequently including ISBN or ISSN and LC card number. The *IEEE Publication Bulletin* and the *IEEE Technical Activity Guide* complement the *Index* for the current year.

The *Engineering Index*, produced by Engineering Information, Inc. (Ei), covers select conference proceedings, at the volume level only, as well as journal articles, technical reports, and some monographs. Ei's annual *Publications Indexed for Engineering (PIE)* provides limited bibliographic information of the conferences included. A computer searchable version, *Compendex*, is available through a number of vendors. A complementary service, *Ei Engineering Meetings*, provides information at the paper level and is currently available online through various vendors either as a separate file or as an integral part of Ei's enhanced *Compendex*Plus*. Unfortunately, the print version lasted only one year.

Numerous other subject specific indexing and abstracting services include conference literature sources. Many of these services are computer searchable and often provide the ISSN or ISBN, if available. The more important of these services for engineering, under their online name, include *Aerospace Database, DOE Energy, Fluidex,* and *Metadex.*

ON LEAVING SOME STONES UNTURNED

No matter how hard you search, some references will not lead to published sources. One obvious reason is that the paper was only read at the conference and either no proceedings have been published to date or the paper is not included with those actually published. This situation can be conjectured when the reference indicates only that the paper was "read at," but it also occurs for references that indicate "proc[eedings . . .]." Either way, the reference, based on notes or informally distributed items, typically provides no page number or publisher information. Publication, however, may have occurred subsequent to the author's citation.

Establishing the facts of publication or non-publication can be a long drawn out process.[19] The existence of the conference and its organizers may have to be established through sources such as *MInd, the Meetings Index, Scientific Meetings* or the various sections of *World Meetings*. Unfortunately, while these sources overlap greatly, they fail to give comprehensive coverage overall. Journals and trade magazines list many conferences and meetings not found in these sources, but still provide no guarantee of completeness.[20] The sponsor, when finally known, may have to be contacted. This contact can be easy for academic sponsors and established groups listed in sources such as *Encyclopedia of Associations, Research Centers Directory* or some international counterpart, but very difficult for the ephemeral or obscure groups responsible for some conferences. The author of the paper may have to be located. This determination may be relatively easy for prolific authors or academics by the use of sources such as *Current Contents Address Directory, National Faculty Directory, American Men and Women of Science, Current Research in Britain*, or an appropriate bibliographic index, but very difficult for graduate students or persons in industry. Given the number of sources to consult, some of which are not owned or conveniently located, these strategies quickly become counterproductive to effective service of other users. Convincing the user of the *likely* situation can be extremely difficult. Determining just what the user really needs in order to pursue alternative sources can be just as frustrating. Deciding which stones to turn and which to leave unturned is part of the art.

One final note of concern. Most citations lead to actual publications. Various search strategies using OCLC, for example, will retrieve records for holdings in other libraries. So many forms of cataloging exist, however, that caution must be used before concluding the item is not owned by one's own or a convenient nearby library. Moreover, the complete holdings for many libraries are not listed on the bibliographic utility and thus card catalogs must be checked in addition to the utility. Knowledge of these collections can be a vital asset in deciding which stone to turn.

The citation as given or as amplified in a reasonable amount of time by these suggested strategies provides the basis for searching the catalog. The process may have to be reiterated. Some recommended procedures with caveats follow.

SEARCHING PROCEDURES
(FOR LIBRARY CATALOGS)

1. Author searching.
   a. Name of editor. This technique is generally effective unless the proceedings have been cataloged as a serial, in which case it will fail.
   b. Name of sponsoring organization. This technique generally has the highest success rate, for both serial and monographic cataloging, although for organizations sponsoring large numbers of conferences, the process of searching can be quite tedious. Limiting by date of publication where possible reduces the tedium for monographic cataloging, of course, but misses serially cataloged items. (In OCLC, drop stopwords such as Association, Institute, and some geographic identifiers that precede the first significant word.)
   c. Name of the conference. A relatively effective technique using an author search key, although the conference name is not universally used as a corporate author. In the case of serial cataloging, it can fail if the conference name changes more rapidly than the serial cataloging.

   Searching corporate authors is usually considerably simpler in an author/title card catalog as opposed to an online catalog. When using an online catalog, it is usually necessary to specify which file (author, title, or subject) is being searched. The fact that the corporate author is often identical to the proceedings title (when descriptive) often facilitates the manual search, while complicating the computer assisted search.
2. Title searching. This technique is generally effective only with descriptive volume titles. When words or phrases such as "proceedings" or "papers presented" are part of the title, the search can be quite tedious or inconclusive.
3. Subject searching. This is the technique of last resort, as it is extremely complicated and time-consuming. When author or title searches prove elusive or too tedious, a subject search under the "Congresses" subheading may locate the desired item or a related item that provides clues on a more suitable form of au-

thor or title searching. Choosing the proper subject heading is not always easy, although records found in bibliographic utilities may suggest the most likely ones. Use this strategy only when all others have failed. Even when the desired item still cannot be found, identification of other possibly related conferences is frequently an eye opener for the user who singularly follows only the citations of a given author.

4. Standard Number searching in bibliographic utilities such as OCLC and RLIN.
   a. ISBN. This techniques is very effective unless the proceedings are being cataloged as a serial, in which case it will fail.
   b. ISSN. This technique is very effective unless the individual volumes are being cataloged as monographs, in which case it will fail.
   c. Library of Congress card number. This technique is most useful for the proceedings of a unique or "independent" conference. For serially cataloged proceedings, this technique can be of limited usefulness. It will often bring up 10 to 15 records, some of which may be serial records, and some of which will be monographic records for specific years.

5. Limiting searches by date. This limitation can often be helpful, especially since the date is almost always included in the standard bibliographic citation. There, however, are two problems of which to be aware:
   a. The date given in the citation may often be the date of the conference rather than the date of publication. This problem can be eliminated by limiting the search to the range of years from the year given to date.
   b. As previously discussed, many conferences are cataloged as serials; thus limiting the search by date will eliminate most if not all of the serial records. This problem can be dealt with by searching on all years *prior* to the date given in the citation. In OCLC, this type of search (when performed for a corporate author) would take the following form:

   $$=xxxx,xxx,x/-[year]$$

   Additionally, many important records have only a partial or unspecified date (197u, for example). In OCLC, *any* attempt to limit by date excludes all of these records. The only way to ensure access to such records is either to not limit by date, or to limit the search to no date records:

= xxxx,xxx,x/????

On the other hand, the RLIN system includes all partial or unspecified dates. A search limited to the year 1979, for example, will automatically pick up all 197u records. Nevertheless, one must still take care not to eliminate serial records when limiting by year.

EXAMPLES

The Society of Photo-Optical Instrumentation Engineers, more commonly known since 1982 as SPIE—the International Society for Optical Engineering, publishes some 80 titles a year in its *Proceedings of SPIE* series. A typical item is fully described on the basis of information on its title page as follows:

Digital optical computing, Raymond Arrathoon, chair/editor, sponsored by SPIE—the International Society for Optical Engineering in cooperation with Center for Applied Optics, University of Alabama in Huntsville; Center for Electro-Optics, University of Dayton; Center for Laser Studies, University of Southern California; Institute of Optics, University of Rochester; Laser Association of America; and Optical Sciences Center, University of Arizona. Papers from a conference held 13-14 January, 1987, Los Angeles, CA, *Proceedings of SPIE—the International Society for Optical Engineering*, Bellingham, WA, SPIE—the International Society for Optical Engineering, v. 752, 1987.

Catalogers will also find on the verso of the title page that publication of the papers does not necessarily constitute endorsement by the editors or by SPIE and that copyright is held by the Society of Photo-Optical Instrumentation Engineers, thus creating ambiguity about the proper corporate author name.

Obviously, the information provided is too much to cite. The form of citation recommended by SPIE on the verso of the title page would give, Author(s), "Title of Paper," *Digital Optical Computing*, Raymond Arrathoon, Editor, Proc. SPIE 752, page numbers (1987). Unfortunately, the most valuable information for facilitating access is excluded from the typical citation. In addition to the author(s), title (may be missing), and pages of the individual paper, the most common references contain only the following information:

Proc., SPIE, 752 (1987) or *SPIE*, 752 (1987).

Following established authority files, in the overwhelming majority of catalog records, the corporate author is listed as Society of Photo-Optical Instrumentation Engineers. Searching OCLC or a catalog containing all the entries for a year can be quite tedious, unless they can be browsed in numerical order. It is important to note that year of publication does not follow exactly the volume number sequence. Searching under the corporate author name beginning "SPIE — The International Society," under the title beginning *Proceedings of SPIE*, or under the author/title forms "SPIE, proc" and "Phot, proc" retrieves only a few scattered post 1982 records in OCLC. Searching the title *Proceedings of SPIE* in NOTIS, the online catalog system in use at Wayne State University and several other libraries in Southeast Michigan, retrieves nearly 400 records, with other libraries in the region holding SPIE proceedings about to enter their records.[21] The current design of NOTIS does not display the volume number in the list of truncated records. Only the titles (in alphabetical order) and year of publication are given, each of which must be examined to find the desired volume. Once the editor or the distinctive volume title is known from INSPEC or other secondary source, searching OCLC or NOTIS presents no problem for monographic cataloging. The small number of libraries that use only overall serial cataloging in OCLC tend to shelve items together in volume number sequence, thereby overcoming the problem for their users. Document delivery services with online access to such serials holdings can also determine if the desired volume is listed.

The inconsistent use of a conference name as both title and corporate author can be illustrated with the Colloquium on Algebra, Combinatorics and Logic in Computer Science held in Gyor, Hungary, Sept. 12-16, 1983. It was published in 1986 by North-Holland under the title *Algebra, Combinatorics and Logic in Computer Science*, edited by J. Demetrovics, G. Katona, and A. Solomaa. A title search beginning *Algebra, Combinatorics, and Logic*/1986 in OCLC retrieves two records with holdings. The Library of Congress record used by about 60 libraries is also retrieved by that title cast as a corporate author. The corporate author search required to retrieve the other record used by about 30 libraries begins Colloquium on Algebra.

Many citations are extremely terse, satisfying thereby the editor and aggravating the librarian. In the following example, from an IEEE conference volume, the name of the first author is listed, together with an acronym of the conference name, a generic title, year, and page number, but neither the title of the paper nor the sponsoring organization is provided:

H. Tanaka, et. al.; ISSCC, Dig. Tech. Paper. (1987) p. 138.

The acronym retrieves nothing in OCLC whether it is used as a corporate author, a title, or in an author/title combination. The generic title, *Digest of technical papers,* retrieves only eight OCLC records when limited to 1987. Browsing these items quickly locates one record that reveals the conference to be the IEEE International Solid-State Circuits Conference. If the generic title had been merely *Proceedings* or other very common term the retrieval and browsing could have been impractical. An author search of a service providing paper level indexing would be more practical, but still tedious if the author were highly productive or the conference relatively obscure. The acronym in this case, however, can be located relatively easily in *Acronyms, Initialisms & Abbreviations Dictionary, Directory of Published Proceedings,* and *Index to IEEE Publications*.

A more general problem concerns retrieving title records utilizing *Proceedings* or other common generic term. This information is often confounded as in the following citation extracts: *Proceedings of the IEEE Autotestcon Conference . . . 1985, 1985 IEEE Autotestcon Proceedings, Proc. 1985 Autotestcon, Conference Record Autotestcon 1985.* The cataloger, with title page at hand, clearly sees the actual corresponding information as Autotestcon '85, *Proceedings*. The more general problem, of course, is the other way around. The citation typically will indicate *Proc.* with the user and reference librarian left to guess whether the full title is the one word *Proceedings* or whether that word merely prefixes a string beginning *Proceedings of* or *Proceedings of the*. Only the cataloger knows for sure, usually. The presence or absence of these little words is highly significant in choosing an efficient retrieval strategy, if Boolean searching is not available.

A citation in another IEEE conference volume requires several more steps for success. Other than name of the author and page number, the only source information provided is *IDGTE* (1983). The acronym finds no match in the usual tools and no paper can be found for the author from 1983 to date. (Users themselves typically do not know what such acronyms stand for in items they request.) The cited author's name is listed in INSPEC as a co-author of an earlier conference paper which, fortunately, proved to be available in the library. One of the references in that paper reveals the relevant name to be Institution of Diesel and Gas Turbine Engineers. An OCLC search of that institution as a corporate author for 1983 and 1984 retrieves two records, with a total of four holding libraries, indicating the likely source as *Generating plant and system*, an international conference . . . London . . . 13 December 1983. If the earlier paper had not been in the collection or the Institution not mentioned therein, the search could have taken very much longer.

Papers "read or presented at" a meeting present problems that often can be resolved. A given author is cited as having read a paper at the Conference on Artificial Intelligence, Austin, Texas, 1984. An author search in ISTP for 1984 and 1985 verifies the source as the 1984 *National* Conference on Artificial Intelligence and provides not only the page numbers, but also ISBN and publisher information.

Information is often garbled. In one example, the authors, paper title, and pages are listed for the IEEE 1986 Monolithic Circuits Symposium. The correct name of that conference according to the IEEE indexes easily proves to be the IEEE 1986 Symposium on Microwave and Millimeterwave Monolithic Circuits. Two of the authors, according to various indexes, have a different paper in the published digest of that conference. A further author search reveals, *evidently,* that the cited paper appears in a different IEEE conference, known in short as GaAs IC 86. Evidently, that is, because the title of the latter paper differs slightly from the one cited, with one critical word omitted. Perhaps, the actual cited paper appears elsewhere, or nowhere at all. *Caveat Emptor.*

CONCLUSION

The difficulty of locating conference proceedings can be minimized by using the proper strategy. Nearly all strategies will, under certain conditions, fail. Searches by editor fail for serially cataloged items, searches by title are troubled by non-descriptive titles. Subject searching is extremely complex and time-consuming, and should should be used only as a last resort. The only strategy which approaches success consistently (perhaps, 80%) is corporate author searching. Even so, this strategy is fraught with difficulty because of uncertainty in determining the form of the name of the corporate author used for cataloging. In order to be successful, the searcher must often try several variations. Clearly, any bibliographic instruction for engineers and scientists, whether given in a classroom setting or at the point of use, must include a component on corporate author searching. This instruction is especially important as the online catalog, which requires the user to specify which file (author, title, or subject) he or she is searching, becomes more and more common.

It is possible that Boolean searching in the online catalog will solve many of the problems connected with accessing conference literature. There are, however, several difficulties. In order for Boolean searching to be effective, the system must have the capability of limitation by field (author, title, subject). Even with this capability, many of the problems of corporate author or title searching will still exist, especially for proceedings volumes with non-descriptive titles. Additionally, in order for Boolean searching to be effective, the system must provide sufficient space for the search to be entered, i.e., there must be enough room provided to list all the important keywords together with appropriate Boolean operators and field delimiters. Ideally, the system should be capable of limiting by date or document type (book, serial, government publication, etc.). A final difficulty is the fact that Boolean searching is extremely time-consuming in terms of computer time. As a result, some libraries may limit this capability to only a few of the public catalog terminals or perhaps only to staff terminals, thus further limiting the usefulness of this capability. The comparatively recent introduction of this capability at most libraries makes it difficult to evaluate. Further investigations should be performed after more time has elapsed.

REFERENCES

1. Manten, A. A. *Symposia and symposium publications*. Amsterdam: Elsevier; 1976.
2. Zamora, Gloria J.; Adamson, Martha C., eds. *Conference literature, its role in the distribution of information: proceedings of the Workshop on Conference Literature in Science and Technology*. 1980, May 1-3, Albuquerque, NM. Marlton, NJ: Learned Information; 1981.
3. Cole, Jim E. Conference publications: serials or monographs? *Library Resources & Technical Services*. 22(2): 168-73; 1978 Spring.
4. Unsworth, Michael E. Treating IEEE conference publications as serials. *Library Resources & Technical Services*. 27(2): 221-24; 1983 April/June.
5. Johnson, Karl E. IEEE conference publications in libraries. *Library Resources & Technical Services*. 28(4): 308-14; 1984 October/December.
6. White, Phillip M.; Breeze, Jerry W. Verifying conference proceedings. *Research Strategies*. 5(4): 191-96; 1987 Fall.
7. Brewer, D. F. Weighing words in conference proceedings. *Nature*. 253: 666; 1975 Feb. 20.
8. Manten (ref. 1): pp. 17-25.
9. Bell, Helen C.; Schultis, G. Ann. Acquiring conference papers through interlibrary loan service. In: ref. 2, pp. 118-47.
10. An interesting attempt to document the shortcomings of a class of biomedical conferences is found in: Funk, Mark E.; Reid, Carolyn Anne. The usefulness of monographic proceedings. *Bulletin of the Medical Library Association*. 76(1): 14-21; 1988 January.
11. Rowley, John C. The conference literature—savory or acrid? In: ref. 2, pp. 11-20.
12. A different perspective on the issues discussed here and an excellent summary of search strategies for alternative forms of publication is found in: Bates, Marcia J. Locating elusive science information—some search techniques. *Special Libraries*. 75(2): 114-20; 1984 April.
13. Zweben, Stuart H., East Central Regional Representative, Association for

Computing Machinery. [Open letter to ACM members in the East Central Region.] 1988 Spring, 4 leaves.

14. Bell and Schultis (ref. 7): p. 120.

15. Kacena, Carolyn. AACR-2, conferences, & you. In: ref. 2, pp. 180-91. AACR-2 section 24.7 discusses the cataloging rules for conference proceedings in some depth. Other important sections dealing with the determination of corporate authority and title include 21.1B1, 24.3F, 26.3, and 1.1B. Problems arise when a recurring conference or its proceedings undergo a title change. Such changes, while usually reflected in library catalogs, are frequently *not* reflected in lists of cited references. Additionally, most authors citing conference papers are not as rigorous in their standards as catalogers.

16. A discussion of the techniques for searching these bibliographic databases is beyond the scope of this paper. Excellent, if somewhat dated, summaries are found in the following references. Hintner, Jo Nell. Cataloging and finding conference publications using OCLC. In: ref. 2, pp. 192-202. Spurrier, Laura J. Use of RLIN in cataloging conference literature. In: ref. 2, pp. 203-17.

17. Chillag, John P. 120,000 conference proceedings from stock: the conference collection and database at the British Library Lending Division. In: ref. 2, pp. 148-57.

18. Spiegel, Martha R. Identification and verification of proceedings information. In: ref. 2, pp. 65-75.

19. Alldredge, Shirley. Techniques and strategies used by seasoned librarians for the identification and evaluation of incorrect or incomplete conference citations. In: ref. 2, pp. 110-17.

20. Hillyer, Georgiana. Announcements of forthcoming meetings. In: ref. 2, pp 44-51.

21. The situation at Wayne State University is unique, in that there is *one* NOTIS system in use by a network of libraries (the Detroit Area Libraries Network—DALNET). Thus, any search currently will display holdings for all libraries in the network.

ERRATUM

The cover date and copyright page for *Science & Technology Libraries*, Volume 9, Number 1 should read Fall 1988.
The publisher regrets any inconvenience this may have caused the reader.

Publishing of Sci-Tech Conference Proceedings: Viewpoint of an Editor

James L. Smith

SUMMARY. A discussion of the problems and difficulties inherent in the publication of contemporary scientific and technical information based on symposia, meetings or workshops, including the production process and the factors affecting the continued viability of this type of publishing. Other topics include: reviewer response, the publisher/professional society symbiosis, the review type hardcover book and the rapid communication journal, with toxicological and nuclear power examples as to the future.

PRODUCTION SCHEDULES

Books; based on conference proceedings or symposia in science and technology present a number of problems to the commercial publisher in the current situation. For anyone charged with the responsibility for seeing that contributors or conference attendees get their papers in on time and in the desired format, some of the front end problems are immediately apparent. A conference proceeding or symposia is one thing. Often the author of the article or contributor is already under compulsion to meet a deadline by virtue of the fact that he or she must have the paper prepared for presentation at the meeting even though the actual presentation may be done by a proxy. It is another thing for the professional editor to begin with

---

James L. Smith is Senior Editor in the Scientific/Technical division of John Wiley & Sons, Inc., 605 Third Ave., New York, NY 10158-0012. He earned his undergraduate degree at Boston College and did graduate work in English and American Literature at the University of Wisconsin.

© 1989 by The Haworth Press, Inc. All rights reserved.

the deadline imposed by a commercial publisher, to select his/her chapter titles and contributors and by whatever means possible to insure that everyone involved delivers on time.

Once the decision has been made that the symposia or conference proceeding will be published, a fast production schedule is generally desirable. The more specialized the meeting/symposia the more likely that any commercial publication possibilities for the book (be it paperback or hardcover) will be limited, and the operative principle will be to get the material published quickly to take advantage of the topical nature of the material, which often has a very short life and in the worst cases (from a commerical point of view) limited to a mere percentage of the original conference attendees. The explosion in sci-tech information means more and more meetings and the possible publication of more and more conference proceedings. As the sheer number of conference proceedings has expanded the commercial possibilities have contracted and nowadays commercial publishers (certainly the larger ones) must take a hard look before deciding to publish a given work.

This is not to say that the situation is hopeless, indeed far from it. The thirst for scientific and technical information can still be satisfied in this area and yield the profits required by the commercial publisher to continue to produce quality work. As with any enterprise involving people, success begins and ends with the skill and dedication of the people involved. The editor's judicious selection of contributors who can be depended upon, his or her skill in motivating, directing and in some cases firmly controlling and in a few cases even rejecting a contributor's work, call for real leadership. Often when a book project begins to go wrong, such as excessive delays, recalcitrant contributors, or a seemingly disparate collection of papers, it turns out that the editor was not really familiar with the people he was dealing with, did not think the project through completely or simply did not keep a firm enough control over his contributors. It is often a simple question of numbers. The more people involved, the more likely that something will go wrong. I have had editors of contributed volumes vow never to go through that again. The next book he or she would author alone. At least this way the individual can control the situation.

My experience has been that the single most difficult problem with contributed books is the failure of a key contributor to deliver on time. I say "key" contributor because it sometimes happens (albeit rarely) that one can proceed lacking a chapter or two, which were never done, without doing real violence to the book. What more often seems to be the case however, is that the entire project is delayed or thrown into jeopardy altogether for lack of certain cornerstone contributions. The publisher can help the professional editor in a number of very important ways.

Once the general configuration of the book has been decided (hardcover, softcover, estimated number of book pages, and the all important delivery date) a separate contract is signed with the professional or outside editor. After fully executing this document the editor will supply to the publisher: chapter titles, full mailing addresses for the contributors and the estimated number of book pages for each contributor since the contributors are generally compensated either on a flat fee per page basis or with a royalty based on his/her contribution relative to the total number of pages in the book. Each contributor will then be asked to sign an agreement with the publisher to deliver his/her chapter to the editor by a certain date. I try to have the contributors get their material to the editor three months before the editor is due to submit the material to me at the publisher's. This gives the professional editor a three month "window" to edit the material before sending the completed manuscript to the publisher ready to go to production. One extremely important detail that must not be overlooked when sending out contributor contracts is to be sure that each contributor knows exactly what is expected of him/her. Most publishers provide a checklist/stylesheet or *Guide to Contributors*, which explains how to handle display material, illustrations and references. This document is necessarily not very detailed, but nevertheless it is invaluable to contributors particularly those people who may be undergoing this experience for the first time.

MARKET OUTLOOK

Considering that even a moderately sized book of 300 to 400 pages may take nine months from the receipt of the completed manuscript to bound books in the warehouse (in some cases even more) the nature of the published material must be balanced against this time frame. This is particularly true in the case of sci-tech material. It becomes critical in the case of an important meeting where dramatic scientific or technical advancements may be announced. This long delay may simply be unacceptable to the scientific community and indeed to the publisher as well, since the market may have evaporated by the time this type of book is published. It is for this reason primarily that commercial publishers favor the meeting/symposia which is of the more general "reviewer" variety, thus insuring that the market will be as broad as it can be within the context of the science or technology under discussion.

The simple question of topicality and the risk of dated information must be faced squarely by the editor/publisher in determining whether or not to proceed. It is common to read in post-publication reviews, for example, that the references in a 1988 book stop in 1985. This is particularly galling to reviewer when, for example, he had a paper published in 1986, 1987 or 1988, which is not listed in the references. Reviewers often choose to ignore or simply don't know that a book may take up to a year to produce and in that year of course, the state-of-the-art is not standing still. It gives me pleasure as an editor of a hardcover book to read in the published reviews that the references are "thorough" or "up-to-date" or "complete." With the technology of hardcover book publication, this is as good as it gets in that department.

There are ways to speed up the process of course, sticking with the example of the hardcover book, such as demanding completely camera-ready copy (manuscript and illustrations) from the contributors, doing no (or very little) copy-editing in-house and skipping the galley stage and going directly to pages. All three potential steps, while saving time, involve some risk in terms of an unacceptable level of errors, which results in negative reviewer commentary or worse still, a "quick and dirty" job which looks it. This results in bad reviews as well. Often the time, care and money that the publisher insists on lavishing on a contributed book from a symposium, risks the whole project, since the market quickly fades while the publisher has a reputation for quality work to protect and will not cut corners. The right combination of review type material, well produced and carefully edited, will continue to have a market long beyond the original meeting or symposium however, and I have indicated before that the situation relative to commercial publication of this material is currently not very dynamic but is by no means moribund.

The attitude of contributors toward publication of his/her article in a hardcover book as opposed to the journal situation is, I think, interesting. In many ways the two are quite similar. Generally, the contributor is entitled to twenty copies of the reprint (perhaps a better word is "preprint," since the publisher generally overuns the appropriate amount at the printer and sends these out simultaneously or even prior to publication of the book) and most contributors seem to take publication in a hardcover book as somehow more prestigious than journal publication. The assumption is that somehow the market for the book is broader than the journal and, of course, the demand for copies of reprints on or shortly after publication is a good barometer of how the book will sell. Both books and journals are extremely important in sci-tech publishing of course, and it is a continuing cause of concern among the publishers of this material to achieve the mix that the market demands.

REVIEW TYPE PUBLICATIONS

This is a good time to discuss the continued viability of this type of publication. I have already discussed some of the mechanical problems inherent in producing this material, but what is the situation generally in these days of extremely rapid growth in sci-tech information? In my view the serial: "Advances in" type of publishing will continue to serve a real need in the sci-tech community. These review type articles, assembled and published as hardcover books on the average of one per year, continue to be invaluable to scientists who need to stay abreast of things in their field without the necessity of sorting through many specialized journals. Two examples that come to mind from chemistry are: *Advances In Chemical Physics*, edited by Prigogine and Rice and *Progress In Inorganic Chemistry*, edited by Lippard.

We might balance these "Advances in" books against traditional journal publishing or the more "rapid communication" type of subscription publication (newsletters, etc.) which is expanding rapidly in the sci-tech area these days. All of these serve specific needs depending on the type of information being presented. An example of what I call a hybrid—a relatively expensive hardcover book involving many contributors which nevertheless deals with a topic which has a great deal of current scientific interest would be: *Toxic Contaminants and Ecosystem Health: A Great Lakes Focus*, edited by Marlene S. Evans and published by John Wiley & Sons. This book is 602 pages and sells for $99.95. The book is Volume #21 in an ongoing series: *Advances In Environmental Science and Toxicology* with Jerome O. Nriagu the series editor.

The book contains thirty chapters with forty-four contributors involved. Each chapter opening has a table of contents and each chapter has a summary and conclusions as well, of course, as complete references. The index runs to eighteen single-spaced, double-columned pages. While each chapter is self-contained, together they go to make up a serious thorough analysis of the contamination of the Great Lakes, a subject which is much in the news these days, and by no means limited to the attention of concerned scientists. It is interesting to note that this imposing book began as a symposium workshop organized by the *Health of Aquatic Communities Task Force* and sponsored by the *Science Advisory Board* of the *International Joint Commission* and the *American Society of Limnology and Oceanography*. The information could have appeared in another form—spread through a number of journals for example, but the publisher (and it is hoped that the scientific community will agree) believes that this is the most effective way to package and deliver the information.

The semi-static review type article is still compatible with publication in the hardcover book format, even in an area of science as dynamic as toxicology. Most sci-tech publishers nowadays have a mix of journals, books, subscription-based materials and databases. The fundamental motive for the sci-tech publisher is still to provide the information in the most efficient and profitable format. That this turns out to be primarily (mostly hardcover) books will not surprise the sci-tech librarian.

I have repeatedly stressed the commercial aspect of this type of publishing. Profits are threatened by the sheer number of publications in the sci-tech field, and one effective solution is the symbiosis that sometimes exists between the commercial publisher and the professional society. The professional society may underwrite a publication with financial support, contract to purchase a number of copies at a reduced price, maintain a series under the editorial control of the society, or simply lend moral support for publication through peer reviewing. The bottom line is dramatically improved for the publisher when the professional society agrees to take a percentage of the first printing. In fact, this can on occasion be a make or break situation. In other words, without the guaranteed sale to the professional society there would not be enough in it for the publisher to proceed.

FUTURE OUTLOOK

I am convinced that there is still a role for the publication of these symposia/meeting abstracts or workshops in hardcover. On one hand the market share seems to be getting smaller in the face of, or perhaps, because of the tremendous expansion of information in sci-tech topics. On the other hand, the growth of information itself is an opportunity. Some of the concerned scientists who read the cover story on the pollution of the Great Lakes in a recent issue of *Chemical & Engineering News* may well be stimulated to read further and purchase a copy of Evans, and it may even come to pass that Evans is reviewed (it is hoped favorably) in *Chemical & Engineering News*.

It has been said that the analytical thrust of contemporary science leads to gathering of more and more data with the answers to questions leading to more questions. One feels the periodic need to review the state-of-the-art, confirm assumptions or discard others, reset oneself and then proceed anew. The single carefully edited contributed volume is still the best vehicle for achieving this. Things are rarely what they seem. After Chernobyl and Three Mile Island, for example, one might assume that the nuclear power reactor situation is moribund and, in fact, not good in the U.S. at present, but again the situation is fluid. Engineers have been working on designs for efficient and safe reactors. Nuclear power is still the best answer to our future energy needs and other industrialized nations (France, Italy, Spain and the Scandinavian countries, for example) are committed to nuclear power for a large share of their future energy requirements.

The point I am making here is that using the nuclear power reactor situation as an example, one might expect that there will be a renaissance in the science and technology of nuclear reactors with a corresponding increase in publication. Such indeed seems to be the case, with fundamental engineering being wedded to contemporaneous computer modeling, statistical techniques and the new discipline of human reliability analysis all to achieve the goal of producing nuclear power reactors which are efficient and as safe as it is humanly possible to make them.

The renaissance is proceeding in a humanly predictable way. Scientists and technicians meet, exchange information, publish their findings following these symposia, meetings, conferences and workshops and, where appropriate, commercial publishers become involved with the dissemination of this information. It has been this way for a long time and will remain so. Indeed, as important as the work itself is the "making public" of the information for the betterment of all humanity.

Cataloging Conference Publications: Problems and Issues

Michael S. Borries

SUMMARY. This paper discusses the nature of conference publications, the problems peculiar to them in terms of cataloging, and the effects of the Anglo-American Cataloging Rules (2nd ed.) and the Library of Congress rule interpretations on these problems.

When I began to write this article, I searched in vain for previous articles written on this topic. There may very well be something out there, but I did not find it. In those works which I did check, conference publications received at best only an acknowledgement of their existence. It is usually assumed that they will get cataloged somehow, and so they do, for they are an important element in a science library's collection. But they present unique problems of their own, with which catalogers must cope. It seems worthwhile to review some of the problems I have encountered in their cataloging while here at Columbia.

SERIALS OR MONOGRAPHS

To begin with, conference publications must be dealt with either serially or monographically. Yet they don't fit well into either category, being more like the duckbill platypus—an interesting combination of things. In fact, the *Index to IEEE Publications*[1] and the ANSI standards for bibliographic citations[2] both treat conference publications as a separate category, distinct from serials and mono-

---

Michael S. Borries is a serials cataloger at Columbia University Libraries, 320 Butler Library, New York, NY 10027. He has the MS (Library Science), MPhil and MA degrees from Columbia University.

© 1989 by The Haworth Press, Inc. All rights reserved.

graphs. It may perhaps be useful to review the similarities of conference publications with monographs and serials.

Conference publications which are most similar to monographs are, of course, those which are issued by conferences which meet only once, and never again. But even conferences which are held repeatedly may issue publications which are more monographic than serial in nature. For instance, there are special workshop publications. Or the conference may have a distinctive theme each year or use a different title each year (we will return to these problems later).

On the other hand, conference publications more closely resemble serials in that, while they might have an editor, there certainly is no single author. And the editor may, on occasion, have no connection with the conference or even the scholarly field of the conference, but instead may be supplied by the publisher for purposes of final publication.

Conference publications also resemble serials in that they are collections of articles. If a conference meets regularly, its publications will most likely appear regularly, as a serial usually does. The publication may even contain news about the next conference, again, much like a serial.

TITLE AND NAME CHANGES

We might now usefully list some of the problems that are peculiar to conference publications. The first is the truly remarkable way in which the names of conferences can change.[3] For instance, the International Conference on Systems, Man, and Cybernetics also is called, in some years, the International Conference on Cybernetics and Society, and most recently changed its name to the IEEE International Conference on Systems, Man, and Cybernetics. The Carnahan conferences are an even more horrifying example. In 1971 it was called the Carnahan Conference on Electronic Crime Countermeasures. In 1974, an international conference was held, called the Carnahan and International Crime Countermeasures Conference. By 1976 it had become the Carnahan Conference on Crime Countermeasures. In 1982, it became the Carnahan Conference on Security Technology. In 1983, it became both the International Carnahan Conference on Security Technology and the Conference on Crime Countermeasures and Security. In 1984, it resumed its name from 1982, but in 1986 it resumed its international character. I can remember one instance in which a conference publication which came across my desk listed four conferences as its predecessors, each conference having a completely different name (unfortunately, I cannot remember any of the names).

The other problem in dealing with conferences is the choice of title, and the variations in title. If each conference in a series of numbered conferences has a theme which is clearly printed on the title page, should one choose this as a title and treat the piece monographically, or should one choose instead the more "generic" title ("Proceedings," "Record," etc.) and treat the piece serially? How much emphasis should one give to typography when making this decision? My own experience has been that title page layout is a fairly happenstance affair, with no one giving much thought to questions which plague catalogers, or readers. Even if one chooses the "generic" title, one can be confronted with a bewildering variety from the same conference in different years. For example, in one year, the title of choice might be "Proceedings," in the next, "Record," varied by "Conference Proceedings," "Conference Record," etc., and further varied by the addition or omission of the conference name in its various forms, either in the front or at the end of the title. Sometimes these titles do reflect real variations in publication, since conferences may choose to issue pre-conference or post-conference publications, or both.

Finally, two (or sometimes more) conferences can choose to hold a combined meeting. Sometimes this is a permanent arrangement, but often it is a "once-only" occurrence.

CATALOGING RULES

The *Anglo-American Cataloging Rules*, 2nd edition (hereafter AACR2), directs that if such publications are handled serially, successive entries be used in all the above situations.[4] For the above reasons, the Library of Congress (hereafter LC), in its rule interpretations,[5] directs that conference and exhibition publications should be cataloged as monographs unless the name of the conference and the title can be shown to remain constant over several issues. At Columbia, it has been the preference of the science libraries, and hence of their cataloger, to have conference publications handled serially whenever possible. Let us discuss the advantages and disadvantages of each decision, and, in the process, let me suggest some ways AACR2 might be modified to make the handling of conference publications as serials easier. We are now, of course, discussing publications of those conferences which are held repeatedly, since it can be assumed that publications of conferences which are held only once are handled monographically as a matter of course.

The ease of handling the many variations in conference publications outlined above is the main reason for choosing monographic treatment of conference publications. In addition, it can be assumed that if such publications are handled monographically, there will be a greater number of access points. Conferences held on a regular basis may have one or several sponsoring bodies which remain constant over the years, but often are sponsored by different bodies in different years. Frequently, one encounters a mixed situation, in which one or two bodies are constant sponsors, but others sponsor the conference only occasionally, or only once. The preference in cataloging to limit added entries for such sponsors to three may mean that sponsoring bodies are not given as added entries. The same, of course, is true with editors of these publications. One may question, however, the usefulness of these access points to the majority of readers. The question is complicated by the ANSI standard's preference for editor as main entry in a citation,[6] although AACR2 calls for the conference name itself as the main entry in most cases.[7]

LC's preference for cataloging conference publications monographically also makes it easier for other libraries to follow suit. Cataloging copy for these publications as serials becomes limited. In the RLIN network, copy provided by LC for a conference as a monograph may be transferred from the BOOKS file to the SERIALS file and used as a basis for cataloging, but if this is done, the record must be modified, sometimes drastically.

The primary reason for cataloging conference publications serially at Columbia is that this insures that the publications will shelve together, and this is seen as most desirable from the users' point of view. An added benefit is in the processing of these publications. Provided that there are no changes requiring successive entry, new volumes need only to be added to an existing catalog record, rather than cataloged anew. Such treatment also helps the reader to more easily identify changes in conference names and publishing practice. Most readers do not seem to look for conferences by sponsoring body, distinctive "theme" titles, or editors (although the ANSI standard may change the latter). Readers, in any event, have not complained about not being able to find a conference publication in these ways, but have complained about not finding such publications shelved together.

LC's rule interpretations on title changes in serial publications[8] have helped to ease some of the problems of title changes. These interpretations allow many variations formerly treated as title changes to be treated as title variations which do not require successive entry. Such variations include the addition or omission of a corporate name at the end of a title, the variation of the representation of that name (either appearing in full or in an acronym or initialism), and the occasional variation of title (e.g., the use of the word "Proceedings" in most years, varied in some years by the use of the word "Record"). Since most readers seem to search for conference publications by the name of the conference, such interpretations of the rules would seem to benefit readers. It may be useful to treat additional variations, such as the presence or absence of a conference name at the beginning of a title, in the same way. We might even think about treating some of the changes in conference names in similar fashion.

Finally, a new problem seems to be looming on the horizon. Many journals seem to be publishing conference proceedings in either their regular issues (usually a single issue being devoted to a conference) or in special issues (combined numbers or supplements). If a library wishes to maintain bibliographic control over these publications through its catalog, it must increasingly analyze journals that formerly were not analyzed, even if it chooses to treat these publications monographically. In many cases, it is almost necessary to treat such publications monographically, since proceedings of different meetings of the same conference may appear in different journals, making treatment as subseries impossible.

I hope that this paper has fully outlined the problems facing catalogers who are confronted with these publications and that, discussion of these problems will help in their resolution.

REFERENCES

1. Institute of Electrical and Electronics Engineers, Inc. *1985 Index to IEEE publications*. New York: Institute of Electrical and Electronics Engineers, Inc.; 1986.

2. Mount, Ellis. A national standard for bibliographic references. *Journal of the American Society for Information Science*. 28(1): 3-12; 1977 Jan.

3. Examples cited are from the author's own experience, verified against the Library of Congress authority file available online through the Research Libraries Information Network (RLIN).

4. Gorman, Michael; Winkler, Paul W., eds. *Anglo-American cataloging rules*. 2nd ed. Chicago: American Library Association; 1978: chapter 21, sections 21.2C, 21.3B.

5. Library of Congress. Processing Services. *Cataloging Services Bulletin*. 32: 19; 1986 Spring.

6. Mount, Ellis. A national standard for bibliographic references. *Journal of the American Society for Information Science*. 28(1): 3-12; 1977 Jan. (p. 6-7)

7. Gorman, Michael; Winkler, Paul W., eds. *Anglo-American cataloging rules*. 2nd ed. Chicago: American Library Association; 1978: chapter 21, sections 21.1B2, category d.

8. Library of Congress. Processing Services. *Cataloging Services Bulletin*. 36: 12-14; 1987 Spring.

Coverage of Conference Documents in Scientific Databases: Viewpoint of Cambridge Scientific Abstracts

Jonathan R. L. Sears

SUMMARY. Following an outline of the nature and some problems of conference literature, its treatment by two bibliographic databases — published by Cambridge Scientific Abstracts Conference Papers Index (CPI) and Aquatic Sciences and Fisheries Abstracts (ASFA) — is described, giving some bibliometric data on conference documents in these files.

INTRODUCTION

The presentation of scientific/technical/medical (STM) information at conferences, symposia, meetings and other gatherings is central to its communication to the community of researchers, specialists and related organizations. Credit and recognition for research depends largely upon dissemination and publication of results, and importance is placed upon being first in print. The stages of the scientific publication cycle, which include conference proceedings, technical reports, scientific journals, annual reviews, and treatises or textbooks, are described by Bates, 1984. The first public airing of a piece of research, outside of one's own organization or network of fellow specialists, often takes place at a conference or symposium. The work may first be presented when it is still

---

Jonathan R. L. Sears, is Senior Editor, Cambridge Scientific Abstracts, 7200 Wisconsin Avenue, Bethesda, MD 20814. He received the BSc from University of London in Marine Biology and Genetics and is currently studying expert systems at the University of Maryland.

© 1989 by The Haworth Press, Inc. All rights reserved.

in preliminary form, although a researcher may also summarize several years' work, parts of which have already been published as journal articles. The size of conferences ranges from the smallest of gatherings to the great multimedia events with thousands of attendees, and so many contributions that they must be presented in parallel sessions.

One word which sums up conference information is "diverse" — in terms of the range of subjects covered, types of meetings, publicity, and format and availability of proceedings. All this conference information is collected and subsequently disseminated in many different types of scientific publications. This diversity is one of the main problems of searching the literature of STM conferences — it can be very hard to identify and locate. Scientific conferences are notoriously problematical for cataloging, particularly where the title of a conference is concerned — this may be given in several different forms within the same document (East, 1985).

Many scientific journals exist entirely for the purpose of reporting the proceedings of their respective societies, beginning with the world's oldest continuously published periodical, the *Philosophical Transactions of the Royal Society*, which began publication on 6 March 1665. Other conference proceedings are published in the mainstream of scientific literature within regular journals, or as "special issues" dedicated to a particular conference. Alternatively, proceedings may be published as a single book, either as a unique volume or monograph, or as a continuous series of proceedings volumes, usually annual. Conference proceedings can become part of the core literature of a given field, as in the literature of information retrieval, where four major proceedings (*Online, International Online Information Meeting, National Online Meeting,* and *ASIS Meetings*) have grown to become major sources of information on online retrieval (Hawkins, 1984). The general publication pattern for conference proceedings has been reported by Mills, 1973, and can be summarized as follows:

1. 40% of conference publications are issued as serials
2. 32% of conference publications are issued as separate books
3. 28% of conference publications are published as special issues within serials.

Often, a formally published record of the proceedings is not produced at all, and the only document might be a program listing the titles and authors of papers to be presented. In some cases, the conference record consists simply of an unbound collection of the authors' papers. Single papers presented at conferences may be published in a journal in the normal way, usually citing the details of the conference (name, location, date etc.) at which it was presented. As a general rule, papers published in a proceedings are not published in the same form elsewhere, such as a scientific journal, but contrary to widely held assumptions, the same research results may appear in different form at later stages in the publication cycle (Bates, 1984).

The availability of conference documents can present a problem for the searcher. It is not unusual for the conference record to be restricted to the participants, or limited in distribution, such as to members of a society. Some meetings are convened to serve as a medium to present work which may be tentative or speculative in nature, or as a forum for exploring certain ideas which could be considerably revised and further developed before publication elsewhere. Such papers may be listed with a footnote indicating "Not to be cited without permission of the author."

ACCESSING CONFERENCE DOCUMENTS

Finding out which conferences are to take place or have previously been held, can be difficult and time-consuming. Announcements in scientific journals or by mail are the most common means to publicize conferences, but with so many meetings going on around the world, the task of staying informed is an onerous one. Cambridge Scientific Abstracts of Bethesda, Maryland, publishes some 30 scientific abstracting/indexing journals and their corresponding online databases, some of which are also available on compact disc. Information presented at conferences is recognized by CSA as an important component of scientific literature, and considerable effort is expended upon its collection and inclusion in CSA's subject-oriented databases.

A unique publication reporting research presented at scientific and technical conferences around the world is *Conference Papers Index* (CPI). Unlike most bibliographlc databases, which focus upon a particular subject area, CPI concentrates upon a sector of the literature based upon document type, namely all types of conference materials. Information is derived from final programs, abstracts booklets, published proceedings, and questionnaire responses. Full details of each conference, including name, location, date, sponsors, World Meeting Number and ordering information are provided in a conference locator in each printed issue of CPI. Material is entered into the database within a time frame of up to six months before or after the conference is held; the aim is to provide current information for the user, as well as a retrospective archive. Coverage includes: (a) Engineering—aerospace science/engineering, civil and mechanical engineering, chemistry and chemical engineering, electronics and general engineering and technology, materials science and engineering, nuclear and power engineering; (b) Biology—animal and plant science; (c) Physics, astronomy, geoscience; (d) Mathematics and computer science; (e) Biochemistry, clinical and experimental medicine, pharmacology. CPI includes over one and a quarter million records dating back to 1973, and its wide scope means that material is included on all fields of science/technology and biomedicine; furthermore, many proceedings included in CPI are not indexed in any other database, and this uniqueness contributes to its value as a source of conference information. Statistical details of materials covered in CPI are given below.

Subject Breakdown, Conference Papers Index, 1972-1987

Aerospace sciences and engineering	50,662 records
Animal and plant science	73,260
Biochemistry	115,404
Biology, general	193,702
Chemistry and chemical engineering	200,759
Civil and mechanical engineering	110,846
Clinical medicine	176,712
Electronics engineering	101,336
Experimental medicine	220,835
General engineering and technology	50,467
Geoscience	114,500
Materials science and engineering	86,255

Mathematics and computer science	76,674
Multidisciplinary	23,017
Pharmacology	75,053
Physics and astronomy	196,454
Nuclear and power engineering	89,533
Special categories	338

Breakdown by Year of Conference, 1972-1987

1972	17,386
1973	128,914
1974	129,337
1975	112,032
1976	56,338
1977	116,050
1978	98,938
1979	89,988
1980	98,260
1981	35,875
1982	85,172
1983	64,071
1984	60,377
1985	93,306
1986	61,818
1987	42,894
	1,290,756

Conference Papers Index can be searched online through Dialog Information Services (file 77), Palo Alto, California, and also through European Space Agency Information Retrieval Service (ESA/IRS, ESRIN), Frascati, Rome, Italy. The following fields may be searched: Title of paper; Conference title; Descriptors; Section headings; Section class codes; Author; Corporate source; Conference location; Conference year; Language; and Meeting number. Searchers can be made to retrieve papers within a broad scientific/technical field, papers on a specific subject, papers from a specific conference, or papers by a certain author or corporate source. A variety of output formats are available, including Accession Number, Title and Indexing, Bibliographic Citation and Full Record.

Sample CPI record

FN - DIALOG File 77: CONFERENCE PAPERS INDEX - 73-88/MAY
AN - 88025479
TI - Thermochemical treatment of SEKA solid waste at 100 ATM for conversion to crudes
AU - Taner, F.; Kimyonsen, U.; Boztepe, H.
CT - Alternative Energy Sources, 8th Miami International Conference
MN - 8745048
CL - Miami Beach, FL (USA)
CY - 16 Dec 1987
SP - Clean Energy Research Institute, University of Miami (Florida)
NT - Clean Energy Research Institute, College of Engineering, University of Miami, P.O. Box 248294, Coral Gales, FL 33124 (USA), Abstracts/extended abstracts, 2 vol. set, $125.00;
Proceedings also available
LA - ENGLISH
JA - V16N3
DE - POWER ENGINEERING
SH - POWER ENGINEERING
SC - 8500

As an example of the treatment of conference information in a subject-oriented bibliographic database, the *Aquatic Sciences and Fisheries Abstracts* (ASFA) database covers many different types of documents, and conference literature comprises a relatively high proportion of the database as a whole, approximately 22%. In the aquatic sciences, conference papers are to be found in a variety of sources, including scientific journals, published proceedings, technical reports, grey literature and items with limited distribution. Some 124 serials in the aquatic sciences alone are dedicated to the proceedings of various meetings worldwide. The policy for ASFA is to catalog and index each individual (analytical) contribution rather than just a single (monographic) entry for the whole conference. Items are not entered in ASFA in advance of the conference.

The worldwide Aquatic Sciences and Fisheries Information System (ASFIS) network of agencies, coordinated by the Food and Agriculture Organization (FAO), Rome, actively collects, catalogs and indexes all types of documents, including conference materials, relevant to the aquatic sciences, and channels these into the ASFA database.

Another ASFIS publication dealing with conferences, the *ASFIS Conference and Meetings Schedule*, is included with *Marine Science Contents Tables* and *Freshwater and Aquaculture Contents Tables*, published by FAO. The Meetings Register gives monthly listings of forthcoming conferences in the aquatic sciences/fisheries area.

Breakdown of Conference Information in ASFA by Language of origin

Language	Whole file	Conferences only
Arabic	154 records	96 records
Bulgarian	173	14
Chinese	1,977	105
Czech	333	3
Danish	81	6
Dutch	198	0
English	210,140	48,072
Estonian	11	0
Finnish	80	8
French	14,665	3,515
German	6,324	473
Greek	29	0
Hebrew	91	3
Hungarian	43	3
Italian	1,955	703
Japanese	4,628	274
Korean	837	0
Macedonian	9	6
Norwegian	533	6
Polish	380	2
Portuguese	1,380	197

Romanian	72	0
Russian	8,349	242
Slovak	2	0
Slovenian	3	0
Spanish	6,335	2,018
Swedish	302	32
Turkish	33	3
Ukrainian	24	0

Conference materials in ASFA by Subject Area, 1976-

	Whole file	Conferences only
Biological sciences/living resources	192,390	39,156
Physical sciences/non-living resources	96,941	26,092

Conference Materials in ASFA by Conference Year, 1976-1987

1976	2996
1977	4522
1978	5230
1979	5513
1980	5378
1981	5150
1982	5286
1983	6568
1984	4366
1985	3745
1986	2844
1987	643

Conference Information in ASFA by Document Type

Document Type	Whole File	Conferences only
Book/Monograph	69,981	44,026

Journal	174,895	11,027
Report	14,927	1,740

The Book/Monograph category above unfortunately does not distinguish single volumes from special monographic issues of journals, which therefore restricts any accurate comparison with the 1973 data of Mills.

The ASFA database is available online through the following systems: Dialog Information Services (file 44), Palo Alto, California; BRS Information Technologies, Latham, New York; European Space Agency Information Retrieval Service (ESA/IRS, ESRIN), Frascati, Rome, Italy; CAN/OLE, Canada Institute for Scientific and Technical Information (CISTI), Ottawa, Canada; DIMDI, Cologne, F. R. Germany; and IFREMER, Brest, France.

The ASFA database is also available on compact disc.

Searchable fields include Title; Abstract; Descriptors; Environment; Identifiers; Section heading codes; Author; Conference title; Conference location; Conference year; Corporate source, Document type; Journal announcement; Journal name/Source publication; Language; Summary language; Publication year; Publisher; Identifying number (ISBN, ISSN, report no. etc.).

Sample ASFA record

1809102 118-09102
TITLE: Production of halibut fry (Hippoglossus hippoglossus) in silos.
CONF: Counc. Meet of the Int. Counc. for the Exploration of the Sea (Santander (Spain)) (1 Oct 1987)
AUTHOR: Rabben, H.; Jelmert, A.; Huse, I.
CORP. SOURCE: Inst. Mar. Res., Austevoll Mar. Aquacult. Stn., N-5392 Storeboe, Norway
PUBL: ICES, COPENHAGEN (DENMARK), 1987, 10 pp.
LANGUAGES: English
SUMMARY LANGUAGES: English
Only available from the author.
DOC. TYPE: Conference; Book
REPORT NO.: ICES-CM-1987/F:42
JOURNAL ANNOUNCEMENT: 8806

ABSTRACT: Silos with conical bottoms and a volume of approx. 3.5m super (3) are tested as storing units for halibut (Hippoglossus hippoglossus) yolk-sac larvae. The silos were run in three different ways: A: Stagnant water with a saltplug till day 10 and later slow upwelling, B: Continuous upwelling, and C: Stagnant with saltplug. High survivals in the silos with constant renewal of water (as a slow upstream) were observed. A negative effect of the saltplug on yolk-sac larvae the second week after hatching was clearly demonstrated.
DESCRIPTORS: rearing; silo culture; survival
ENVIRONMENT: Marine
SECTION HEADING CODES: 1582

CONCLUSION

Conference materials constitute a significant portion of the scientific literature, and frequently contain information not available elsewhere, or early results presented ahead of more formal scientific publications. Proceedings may be published concurrently with the meeting, or they may take up to two or more years to appear, thus searches for published proceedings may need to cover several years. Also, the substantive information of a paper presented at a conference may differ from the version which appears in the published proceedings — if published after the conference, more results may have been added in the interim; if published at the time of the conference, the paper was probably prepared months in advance, and more results may have been available at the time of the meeting. Papers may also be withdrawn or substituted prior to the meeting, and the proceedings may or may not reflect the actual papers presented. Despite these drawbacks, proceedings can be an effective source of information, often as an alternative when journal literature on a subject is unavailable. Services such as Conference Papers Index and Aquatic Sciences and Fisheries Abstracts provide access to meetings and individual articles contained within proceedings. A flexible approach to searching, e.g., by using variants of conference names, conference year, and key words in document titles or sponsoring agency names, will improve search results.

REFERENCES

Bates, M.J. Locating elusive science information: some search techniques. *Special Libraries*. 75(2):114-120; 1984.

East, J.W. Citations to conference papers and the implications for cataloging. *Library Resources and Technical Services*. 29(2):189-194; 1985.

Hawkins, D.T. The literature of online information retrieval: an update. *Online Review*. 8(2):153-164; 1984.

Mills, P.R. Characteristics of published conference proceedings. *Journal of Documentation*. 29:36-50; 1973.

ACKNOWLEDGMENTS

I acknowledge with thanks the kind review of this paper by Angela HiHi and Evelyn Beck of CSA.

Secondary Publisher Coverage of Engineering Conference Papers: Viewpoint of Engineering Information, Inc.

Gloria Moline

SUMMARY. Engineering Information, Inc. (Ei) is a secondary publisher which has provided access to the engineering conference literature via indexes and abstracts since its founding in 1884. The subject scope, sponsors, publishers, formats and volume of the conference literature covered by Ei are described, problems related to acquisition are discussed and future challenges are presented.

INTRODUCTION

The role of conferences, symposia and other meetings in the transfer of scientific and technical information is well documented. The importance of the published proceedings and papers which result from conferences in the field of engineering is well accepted. However, the role of the secondary publisher (variously described as "abstracting and indexing service," "database producer," etc.) in providing access to the vast body of engineering conference literature is less well recognized. Secondary services recognized the need to provide access to conferences even when the number of published engineering conference papers was relatively small, as

---

Gloria Moline is Manager of the Database Production Division of Engineering Information, Inc., 345 East 47th Street, New York, NY 10017. She received the BA in Liberal Arts from the University of Chicago and the MA in Librarianship from San Jose State University.

© 1989 by The Haworth Press, Inc. All rights reserved.

illustrated in the preface to the first volume of the *Descriptive Index of Current Engineering Literature*,[1] published in 1892 and precursor of *The Engineering Index*.

> Although there are over eleven (11) thousand notes and cross references in this list, no claim is made for its completeness, even for the period covered by it. It is thought to contain, however, nearly all periodical, society, and fragmentary matter of permanent value not only for the period 1884 to July 1891, inclusive, but a great deal which appeared earlier. Thus the entire proceedings of the American Society of Civil Engineers, of the American Society of Mechanical Engineers, and of the Association of Engineering Societies, have been indexed so far as they seemed deserving.

This paper will address the subject based on the experience of a single secondary publisher. Engineering Information, Inc. (Ei) is an independent, not-for-profit information service which provides indexes and abstracts of conference proceedings and papers (and other forms of published literature) in both print and electronic form.

Ei indexes conference proceedings in the printed *The Engineering Index® Monthly*, and *The Engineering Index® Annual*. Comprehensive coverage of individual conference papers, as well as reviews of all proceedings, can be found online in the Ei ENGINEERING MEETINGS® and, beginning in 1988, in the COMPENDEX®*PLUS databases.

CHARACTERISTICS OF THE ENGINEERING CONFERENCE LITERATURE COVERED BY Ei

Subject Scope

Conferences are held and papers are published worldwide in virtually all of the disciplines and related subject areas of engineering. Ei's scope covers the breadth of subject areas in engineering reflected by the conferences themselves.

Figure 1 shows the major areas of engineering covered in the Ei databases; Figure 2 indicates the specific application areas covered. In addition, multidisciplinary areas such as energy and transportation are covered, and management issues and engineering education are also well represented.

Sponsors and Publishers

Engineering conferences are sponsored and published by a wide variety of organizations throughout the world. These publishers include professional societies (e.g., American Institute of Chemical Engineers, American Institute of Mining, Metallurgical and Petroleum Engineers, American Society of Civil Engineers, American Society of Mechanical Engineers, Institute of Electrical and Electronics Engineers); research institutions (e.g., Australian Road Research Institute, Electric Power Research Institute, Environment Research Institute of Michigan, Illinois Institute of Technology); corporations (e.g., AT&T, Exxon, General Motors, IBM, Siemens); commercial publishers (e.g., Hemisphere Publishing Corp., Elsevier Science Publishing Co., Pergamon Press); and, in some cases, by individuals.

```
Chemical Engineering

Civil Engineering

Electrical and Electronics Engineering including

   Computers and Control

Mechanical Engineering

Mining and Metallurgical Engineering including

   Petroleum Engineering and Fuel Technology
```

FIGURE 1. Major Engineering Areas

```
Aerospace Engineering
Agricultural Engineering
Automotive Engineering
Bioengineering
Ceramics and Composites Engineering
Environmental Engineering
Food Engineering
Industrial Engineering
Instrumentation
Materials Science
Nuclear Engineering
```
FIGURE 2. Application Areas

Formats

The papers which result are distributed in an almost infinite variety: from individual preprints to formal multi-volume sets. Some conference proceedings are published in single or multiple issues of journals; others as monographs or parts of monographic series. Still others are issued without cover or title page in an author-typed, stapled format, lacking identification except perhaps for a footnote stating the name and location and/or date of the meeting.

Time Lag

Timely reporting of research and development results is an acknowledged advantage of the engineering conference, but publication of the proceedings of conferences may sometimes be delayed many months (even years). Acquisition and processing by the secondary publisher can add many months to the publication date, resulting in the following circumstance: a conference held late in 1985 results in published proceedings issued late in 1986 which is acquired by a secondary service in mid-1987, abstracted and indexed in a first-in, first-out sequence and made available via its indexes in early 1988. More than two years will then have elapsed between the time the research paper was delivered and the time access to it has been provided by the secondary service.

Fortunately, this occurrence is the exception rather than the rule; the average time lag at Ei is three to six months. When the primary publisher has issued the preprints or the proceedings volume in advance of the conference and quickly made them available to Ei, we have been able to provide access to the papers shortly after their delivery at the meeting.

Volume of Papers

The current annual volume of published engineering conference papers has been estimated at well over 150,000 and appears to be growing along with the technical and financial success of the conferences themselves as vehicles of technology transfer. Ei's coverage of conference papers over the years has risen dramatically in an attempt to keep up with the burgeoning literature. In fact, Ei's annual coverage of conference proceedings has more than doubled in eleven years; coverage of individual papers from those conferences has increased almost 4 1/2 times. Table 1 illustrates the growth in Ei's coverage of proceedings and papers and compares the volume of conference papers with that of other literature in Ei's print and electronic products over the period 1977-1987.

The average number of papers per proceedings volume has varied year to year from thirty-five to sixty-five, but the range varies from as few as three to as many as five hundred or more papers per proceedings. The cost of acquiring proceedings varies greatly as well—some are provided as part of the conference registration; oth-

TABLE 1
GROWTH OF Ei's CONFERENCE COVERAGE

Database Year	Number Conferences	Conference Papers	Other Publications, (Journal Articles, Reports, Monographs)
1977	820	20,900	74,088
1978	891	22,581	72,803
1979	886	27,404	72,532
1980	886	31,509	63,973
1981	1124	32,943	72,601
1982	1875	65,214	114,776
1983	1644	94,874	106,795
1984	1546	100,150	140,029
1985	1897	85,067	127,136
1986	1680	90,044	130,208
1987	1820	90,396	130,327

ers cost several hundred dollars. We have found at Ei that the current average price of a conference proceedings is $140.

IDENTIFYING, SELECTING
AND ORDERING CONFERENCE PROCEEDINGS

The secondary publisher shares with the scientific and technical library the challenge of identifying high quality conference proceedings which will be of lasting value to their respective clients. Ei makes use of traditional reference tools;[2-6] has had a long-standing cooperative relationship with the Engineering Societies Library (ESL); has developed excellent working relationships with major engineering societies, commercial publishers and research institutes; and, relies heavily on the advice of its advisory council and user groups.

As has been indicated, the published conference literature is larger in volume than Ei's present ability to cover it. Limitations in budget, staff and space, as well as the users' ability to pay for what would be a huge database, result in the need for selectivity. Ei has developed a complex set of selection criteria, including the factors of subject area, technical level, publisher, age, etc., which it applies to the conference proceedings received.

Once identified, Ei may establish standing orders with societies and other publishers for direct receipt of all of their relevant conference proceedings; may borrow conference publications from ESL; or, may request individual titles from the publisher on the basis of announcements, ads and other alerting mechanisms. For the latter, a long wait, repeated correspondence and substantial cost can sometimes result.

The Ei Record

Once selected, all of the technical and professional papers in the proceedings are indexed, abstracted, and provided with comprehensive bibliographic citations. This information becomes the Ei "record." For each proceedings a review record is prepared which describes the content of the proceedings as a whole, indicates the number of papers included and provides an Ei-generated conference code number by which all papers from the conference can be conveniently identified in a computer search.

Obviously, the purpose of the secondary publisher is to provide access to the literature, but not to substitute for it. Therefore, Ei must supply in each record it produces enough information to allow the searcher to determine (1) if the full paper can meet the information need and, if so, (2) how to obtain that paper.

To identify and assist in evaluating the relevance of a given paper to one's search questions, Ei provides in COMPENDEX*PLUS and the Ei ENGINEERING MEETINGS databases, the information listed in Table 2.

Sample records from COMPENDEX*PLUS on DIALOG are seen in Figures 3 and 4, illustrating the information typically provided in a proceedings review record and an individual paper from the same conference.

Document Delivery

Assuming that the many access points provided in the Ei record have led to the identification of one or more relevant conference papers, the next challenge becomes one of locating the full text.

Providing the hard copy of conference papers has been cited by librarians and other searchers as one of the most frustrating, time-consuming, and frequently fruitless activities they can be involved in. They describe the conference literature as "ephemeral," "fugitive" and "elusive," and with good reason. Preprints may be housed by the publisher and by some libraries for only a brief period of time, after which they are discarded. Some proceedings are printed in short runs, for distribution solely to meeting attendees and perhaps to a few selected libraries. Some proceedings are too costly to be acquired by many libraries. Bibliographic citation and control are complicated by the diversity of formats in which proceedings are presented, as well as by the all-too-common publisher practice of varying the title of serial conference publications from year to year. Because of their inconsistencies and the varying quality of bibliographic detail provided, conference proceedings may be

TABLE 2
Ei CONFERENCE DATA ELEMENTS

Pertaining to the Conference and the Proceedings Publication	Pertaining to the Individual Paper
Conference Name	Title
Conference Location	Author(s)
Conference Date	Affiliation of first Author
Conference Sponsors	Abstract
Proceedings Title	Controlled Vocabulary
Series Title, Volume, Number	Free Language Terms
Editor(s)	Classification Code

TABLE 2 (continued)

Pertaining to the Conference and the Proceedings Publication	Pertaining to the Individual Paper
Publisher Name and Location	Language
Date of Publication	Pagination
Availability	
Collation	
ISSN/ISBN	
Coden	
Ei Assigned Conference Number	

FIGURE 3. Conference Proceedings Review Record

```
FN- DIALOG COMPENDEX FILE 8|
AN- 02554196|
AN- <EI MONTHLY> EIM8803-017093|
TI- CONSTITUTIVE MODELING FOR NONTRADITIONAL MATERIALS.|
AU- Stokes, V. K. (Ed.); Krajcinovic, D. (Ed.)|
CS- GE, Corporate Research & Development|
CT- Constitutive Modeling for Nontraditional Materials.
CL- Boston, MA, USA
CI- Presented at the Winter Annual Meeting of the American Society of
    Mechanical Engineers.|
CD- 1987 Dec 13-18|
SP- ASME, Applied Mechanics Div, New York, NY, USA|
SO- AMD (Symposia Series) (American Society of Mechanical Engineers,
    Applied Mechanics Division) v 85. Publ by ASME, New York, NY, USA 247p|
PY- 1987|
CO- AMDVAS|
SN- 0160-8835|
CN- 10868|
LA- English|
DT- CP; (Conference Proceedings)|
JA- 8803|
AB- This conference proceedings contains 15 papers on research on polymers,
    polymer composites and ceramics. Some of the subjects covered include
    texture, deformation, neck propagation, drawing, lateral strain
    effects, stress-strain behavior, crazes, microdefects and elastic
    properties. Also covered are transformations, microcracking, fracture
    and toughening in ceramics.|
DE- *MATERIALS--*Strain; CERAMIC MATERIALS; POLYMERS; COMPOSITE MATERIALS--
    Fiber Reinforced; STRESSES; FRACTURE MECHANICS|
ID- DEFORMATION; MICROCRACKING; CONSTITUTIVE MODELING; EIREV|
CC- 815  (Plastics & Polymeric Materials); 812  (Ceramics & Refractories)
    ; 421  (Materials Properties); 931  (Applied Physics)|
CC- <GENERAL>81  (CHEMICAL PROCESS INDUSTRIES); 42  (MATERIALS PROPERTIES
    & TESTING); 93  (ENGINEERING PHYSICS)||
```

FIGURE 4. Individual Conference Paper Record

```
FN- DIALOG COMPENDEX FILE 8|
AN- 0255421l|
AN- <EI MONTHLY> EIM8803-017108|
TI- CONSTITUTIVE BEHAVIOR OF CERAMICS: IMPLICATIONS FOR FRACTURE UNDER
    CYCLIC COMPRESSIVE LOADS.|
AU- Suresh, S.|
CS- Brown Univ, Providence, RI, USA|
CT- Constitutive Modeling for Nontraditional Materials.
CL- Boston, MA, USA
CI- Presented at the Winter Annual Meeting of the American Society of
    Mechanical Engineers.|
CD- 1987 Dec 13-18|
SP- ASME, Applied Mechanics Div, New York, NY, USA|
SO- AMD (Symposia Series) (American Society of Mechanical Engineers,
    Applied Mechanics Division) v 85. Publ by ASME, New York, NY, USA p
    233-247|
PY- 1987|
CO- AMDVAS|
SN- 0160-8835|
CN- 10868|
LA- English|
DT- PA; (Conference Paper)|
JA- 8803|
```

AB- This paper examines constitutive models for microcracking and transformation toughened ceramics with the objective of developing a general theory of fracture under cyclic loads. A review is presented of the recent experimental observations that the application of cyclic compressive stresses to notched plates of ceramics can lead to stable Mode I fatigue crack growth. A constitutive model for microcracking of brittle solids subjected to cyclic compression is discussed. It is shown through finite element analysis that residual tensile stresses are developed at the notch tip when permanent strains are retained within the microcrack zone upon unloading from the far field compressive stress. This region of residual tension is interpreted to be the driving force for stable Mode I crack growth in notched plates of ceramics stresses in uniaxial cyclic compression. An experimentally-substantiated generalized constitutive model for tranforming ceramics which incorporates both dilatational and shear strains accompanying martensitic transformations is described. This formulation is used to rationalize experimental results on crack growth in transforming ceramics stressed in cyclic compression. (Edited author abstract) 11 refs.|
DE- *CERAMIC MATERIALS--*Fracture; MATHEMATICAL TECHNIQUES--Finite Element Method; STRESSES; FATIGUE OF MATERIALS|
ID- MICROCRACKING; TRANSFORMATION TOUGHENING; CYCLIC COMPRESSIVE STRESS; TRANSFORMATIONS; FATIGUE CRACK GROWTH; CONSTITUTIVE MODELING|
CC- 812 (Ceramics & Refractories); 421 (Materials Properties); 921 (Applied Mathematics)|
CC- <GENERAL>81 (CHEMICAL PROCESS INDUSTRIES); 42 (MATERIALS PROPERTIES & TESTING); 92 (ENGINEERING MATHEMATICS)||
?

difficult to identify and retrieve even if they are present in the library.

To prevent the frustration, to close the gap in the information loop between the information in the paper and the user who needs it, and to meet the stated requirements of its users, in mid-1987 Ei established its on-demand Document Delivery Service (DDS). Through this service Ei is able to provide, in photocopy or facsimile form, virtually every conference paper cited in its databases, at a reasonable price and with a minimum of inconvenience.

CURRENT AND FUTURE CHALLENGES

While Ei would prefer to cover all engineering conference papers published, we understand that it is not currently realistic for us to do so—both our resources and market demand are limiting factors. Selecting "more of the best" in a growing universe of excellent proceedings is both a present and a future challenge.

Remaining current is a continuing challenge: while we cannot control delays in the publication of proceedings, we are continuing to improve our internal operations so that the time it takes to acquire, abstract, index and catalog is shortened. To achieve this goal, we have revamped our production system, eliminated redundancies and enhanced quality control.

In summary, Ei has, since its founding, been committed to providing engineering and related technical information to engineers, scientists, librarians, managers and others. To the extent that engineering conferences continue to provide a fast, informal, effective means of technology transfer and information flow, Ei will continue to provide access to it by the most expeditious means possible.

NOTES

1. *Descriptive index of current engineering literature, Volume I. 1884-1891*. Chicago: Board of Managers of the Association of Engineering Societies; 1892: p.iii.
2. *Forthcoming international and technical conferences*. London: Aslib.

3. *InterDok directory of published proceedings, series SEMT-science/engineering/medicine/technology*. Harrison, NY: InterDok.
4. *The serials directory: an international reference book*. Birmingham: Ebsco; 1986. 3 volumes.
5. *World meetings, outside United States and Canada*. New York: Macmillan.
6. *World meetings, United States and Canada*. New York: Macmillan.

InterDok Corporation Publications for the Identification and Acquisition of the Sci-Tech Conference Proceedings Literature

Bernard B. Baschkin
Karen-Anne Baschkin

SUMMARY. Describes the sources of information about conference proceedings used by the InterDok Corporation, as well as its editorial processes. Gives a description of the scope and features of the indexing and alerting publications of InterDok along with a look at future products.

SOURCES OF INFORMATION

The InterDok Corporation has been involved with conference literature since 1965, when it began publication of *Directory of Published Proceedings*. The goal of the publication was to identify and index proceedings arising out of technical and engineering conferences. Thus having accurate and complete information on such meetings was of vital importance.

The primary sources of information for the publication of conference proceedings are the thousands of societies, institutions and organizations which, on a worldwide basis, are responsible for organizing the conferences, congresses, workshops and symposia,

---

Bernard B. Baschkin is the founder and publisher of InterDok Corporation, 173 Halstead Ave., Harrison, NY 10528. He has the BS in Mechanical Engineering from Syracuse University and the MS in Industrial Management from NYU. Karen-Anne Baschkin is the manager of the conference proceedings acquisitions department at InterDok Corporation. She has the BA in literature.

© 1989 by The Haworth Press, Inc. All rights reserved.

and for arranging for the eventual publication of the proceedings. Not an insignificant number of societies and organizations have only a limited life span, reflecting short-term to medium trends in the various sci-tech disciplines, and/or the national and economic priorities assigned to these areas of developing technology. In identifying these sponsoring organizations, bibliographic tools such as *Encyclopedia of Associations* published by Gale Research Company of Detroit, and parallel reference publications coming out of the Western European industrial nations are utilized. Within the past years, more and more bibliographic data has emerged from Japan, reflecting that country's ever-expanding importance in the fortunes of the world economy. Specific reference is made to the *Japan Directory of Professional Associations*, 1984-1987, published by the Japan Publications Guide Service of Tokyo. InterDok Corporation maintains a library of directories of corporations, societies institutions, colleges and universities which reflect the varied sources of sponsorship of conferences. A more detailed listing of some of our reference material is to be found in Appendix 1.

A secondary source of proceedings information results from library research conducted at several leading sci-tech libraries, both in the United States and abroad. A substantial amount of journal literature from leading engineering and scientific societies provides additional input, though often at the cost of duplication and triplication of raw data. Thus, information coming into InterDok is subject to a substantial amount of filtering and review to ensure the integrity of the individual citations and to eliminate duplication of entries. A most interesting and productive source of conference literature results from exchange agreements with several of the leading Eastern European countries, including libraries in the Soviet Union as well as in the German Democratic Republic. These exchanges not only provide for the proceedings published by these two leading Eastern European countries, but also make available publications arising out of the neighboring Eastern countries, such as Poland and the Balkans.

A final source of information is provided by a number of societies and commercial publishers, who arrange for the transmittal of review copies of their proceedings to ensure prompt and accurate inclusion in the *Directory*.

EDITORAL PROCESSES

The process of preparing conference literature for inclusion in the *Directory of Published Proceedings* is extremely thorough and precise. Many organizations do not verify the information prior to including it in their particular publication. Because of the nature of conferences and the sometimes vagueness of information, it is necessary to verify all key information. If there are any questions as to the validity of the data, the citation is not input into the database until verification has been received by the editorial staff. Once the basic information is prepared, the data is then entered into the system. The various indices are created from this information. The subject-sponsor index is created through the key words of the conference title and by the sponsoring organization names. The location and editor indices index the conference material by the conference location and publication editor respectively.

Although all of the conference material is initially verified, there are constant changes and updates. These changes may be price increases, availability of the publication, new distributors etc. All of these refinements must also be verified. These changes are then reflected in the cumulated volume of the *Directory of Published Proceedings*.

InterDok PUBLICATIONS

Several years after the creation of the original *Directory* coverage was broadened to include the medical and life sciences, at which time the designation SEMT (Science/Engineering/Medicine/Technology) was born. In 1968 a parallel *Directory* was introduced to cover the published proceedings in the Social Sciences and Humanities (thus beginning the SSH series).

A specialized *Directory* identifying the proceedings literature arising out of the broadly based pollution control and ecological disciplines was introduced to subscribers in 1976. The Series SSH continues to be published quarterly; the Series PCE is now an annual volume.

Because of the diverse needs of various libraries and information centers insofar as current awareness was concerned, the Series

SEMT *Directory* was expanded to include also an annual cumulated volume. This permitted the introduction of changes, revisions, updates and corrections, and made available to users an annual edition where a current monthly service was not critical. With the introduction of computerization in the editorial process, it became practical to publish also cumulated indices within a volume year (Series SEMT Cumulated Index Supplement) as well as multi-year cumulations. The most recent 5-year Index in the Series SEMT was published in 1982. The current 5-year Index is tentatively scheduled for production in late 1988.

Commencing in the spring of 1987, InterDok Corporation initiated a major project to:

1. Make substantial improvements in the editorial processing of conference proceedings data and the parallel preparation of the indices.
2. Improve dramatically the typography, permitting the introduction of different type styles and sizes to enhance the appearance and legibility of the published text.

Figures 1 and 2 show several samples of proceedings citations and index entries as presently appearing in the *Directory*, and the new version, which will begin to appear in the various sections of the *Directory* as the new system becomes operative.

A cooperative program with the Sedgewick Printout Systems Company of Princeton, New Jersey, was recently completed and is now in the fine tuning stage. Introduction of the new typography/system is being gradually implemented with a parallel phasing-out of the existing system and processes. Parallel production is anticipated for the remainder of the year, as cumulations of indices and special annual and multi-year cumulated volumes and indices must be completed on the "old" system. Initial production issues of the *Directory* will appear later this year reflecting the new system.

A key change is the ability of the program to immediately generate all indices, including the complex subject/sponsor index. A complete set of all indices for a particular issue of the *Directory* is generated by the computer within an hour or two of completion of the data entry for the basic conference proceedings citations.

A major long-term dividend will be the ability to generate a database permitting the eventual online service so much in demand by existing and potential subscribers.

SUPPORTING SERVICES

As an outgrowth of the extended information network established by InterDok Corporation, a futures meetings information service, *MInd-the Meetings Index*, was introduced in 1984. Published bimonthly, the *Meetings Index* cites approximately 400 future meetings per issue, with the maximum lead-time of about two years. Changes of dates and/or venue are highlighted in subsequent issues of the index. Coverage is on a worldwide basis; approximately 40% of the citations reflect meetings scheduled outside of North America. The inter-relationship between the data incorporated into the *Meetings Index* with the subsequent publication of the *Directory of Published Proceedings* is yet another source of potential information relating to the published proceedings literature. It should be remembered, however, that only approximately 50% of conferences result in the publication of proceedings or a specific unit collection of the papers, reports and discussions. More often than not, publication of the papers will commence months and often years after the conference has concluded.

A parallel service to the *Directory of Published Proceedings* and the *Meetings Index* are various standing order plans for conference proceedings to be furnished to the subscriber. Arrangements can be made for proceedings procurement by subject matter, by specific conference series or by specific society. Complications can arise quickly, as many conferences are co-sponsored by a number of societies each reflecting individual distribution policies and pricing. Orders are also often received as a result of information located in the *Meetings Index*. Here the acquisitions department maintains constant dialogue with the sponsoring organizations to ensure the earliest possible receipt of the required proceedings by the subscriber. On occasion, special requests are received from libraries and information centers for proceedings that have not been included in either the *Directory of Published Proceedings* or the *Meetings Index*. These special requests receive immediate attention.

FIGURE 1. Old

8/76-1355 Acapulco, MEX
World congr. for the Prevention of alcoholism &
drug dependency, ICPA 2nd (Positive alternatives to
false dependencies)
Sp: International Commission for the Prevention of
Alcoholism (ICPA)
Ed: Francis A. Soper
Pub: International Commission for the Prevention of
Alcoholism & Drug Dependency
Report $5.00 1977 Approx. 480p.

10/76-1356 San Antonio, TX, USA
Natl. Health forum, 1976 of the Trinity University
Sp: Trinity University, Center for Continuing
Education in Health Administration
Ti: Cost accountability for health services in the
United States
Ed: E. Gartly Jaco
Pub: Center for Continuing Education in Health
Administration, Trinity University
$3.95 1977 117p.

6/78-1515 Waterloo, IA, USA
SFRA 1978 Natl. conf.
Sp: Science Fiction Research Association (SFRA)
Sp: University of Northern Iowa: Department of
English Language & Literature, & Division of
Extension & Continuing Education
Ed: Thomas J. Remington
Pub: University of Northern Iowa, Department of
English Language & Literature
Selected proceedings $12.50 1979 281p.

12/78-1516 Varanasi, IND
Education & world hunger, IAEWP 2nd World congr.
Sp: International Association of Educators for World
Peace (IAEWP)
Ti: Education & world hunger: educational remedy of
hunger for world peace
Ed: S. N. Prasad
Pub: D. K. Agencies (P) Ltd.
$14.00 1985 (DK-8504-40997) 135p.

```
UNESCO
  Motivation for adult education, European conf.
    2nd: Motivation for adult education                    2/83-1094
  Participate in development, Expert mtg.                 12/79-1522

UNESCO Institute for Education (UIE)
  Motivation for adult education, European conf.
    2nd: Motivation for adult education                    2/83-1094

United Nations Economic Commission for Latin America &
  the Caribbean (ECLAC)
  Caribbean cooperative rice research network, Workshop   8/84-0999

United Nations University (UNU)
  Man in the mangroves: the socio-economic situation of
    human settlements in mangrove forests, Workshop        5/85-0584
  Nouvel ordre economique international: aspects
    commerciaux, technologiques & culturels, Colloq.     10/80-1370

United States & western Europe, Economics & politics of
  industrial policy                                        2/85-0559
```

FIGURE 2. New

12/79-0001 San Francisco, CA, USA
Perspectives on historical linguistics, Conf., at MLA Annual conv.
Sp: Modern Language Association of America (MLA), Language Theory Division
(Amsterdam studies in the theory & history of linguistic science. Ser. IV: Current issues in linguistic theory: ISSN 0304-0763, Vol. 24)
Ed: Winfred P. Lehmann & Yakov Malkiel
Pub: Benjamins (John) B.V.
US Distrib: Benjamins (John) North America, Inc.
$48.00   1982   ISBN 90-272-3516-3   379p.

4/81-0001 Oxford, GBR
Comparative judicial systems: challenging frontiers in conceptual & empirical analysis, Conf.
Sp: International Political Science Association (IPSA), Research Committee for Comparative Judicial Studies
(Advances in political science; 6)
Ed: John Richard Schmidhauser
Pub: Butterworths Publishers, Inc.
$35.00   1987   LC87-13151   ISBN 0-408-03165-4

11/82-0001 Frascati, ITA
Educational research workshop
Sp: Council of Europe (CE)
Ti: New technologies in secondary education
Pub: Swets Publishing Service, Div. of Swets & Zeitlinger, B.V.
Distrib: Hogrefe International, Inc.
Report fl.40($21.50est.)   ISBN 90-265-0455-1   214p.

11/82-0002 San Francisco, CA, USA
Strategic management of operations, OMA 1st Annual winter conf.
Sp: Operations Management Association (OMA)
Ed: Steven Wheelwright, Roger Schroeder, & Jack Meredith
Pub: Operations Management Association
$25.00est.   1983   50p.

Treatment of developmental dyslexia & learning disorders,
 Current concepts in the diagnosis &   4/86-0006

Unequal access to information resources: problems & needs of
 the world's information poor   2/86-0003

Universal grammar & philosophical analysis of language,
 Speculative grammar   10/84-0007

University of Bologna
 Speculative grammar, universal grammar & philosophical analysis
  of language   10/84-0007
 Speculative grammar, universal grammar, & philosophical analysis,
  Sem.   10/84-0007

University of North Carolina at Chapel Hill
 Community health conf., Annual
  8th: Conceptual models of nursing applications in community
   health nursing   5/84-0001

University of Waterloo, Institute for Risk Research
 Risk management for dangerous goods, Workshop   4/86-0007

University research support personnel   9/84-0005

A LOOK AHEAD

In looking ahead, a paramount source of information for research needs is and will continue to be the conference. The medium of the conference is such that it *is* the state-of-the-art for information exchange.

Although there is great demand for the published conference proceedings, there appears to be a development in the nonprint media for the documentation and dissemination of conference literature. There is a supplemental market, currently in development, which utilizes audio and visual tape cassettes. With the advent of the video cassette recorder (VCR), it seems only natural to videotape the conference, thus enabling non-attendees to participate through sight and sound rather than by simply reading the material.

There is also much research and development in the telephone video conferencing system. There are services offered where conferences are transmitted across great distances via satellite telecommunication systems. Because of this recent development in teleconferencing, there can now be long distance involvement in simultaneous meetings. This new form is becoming one of the most important developments in conferencing.

There is a need in North America for the organization of a centralized data source for conference literature. In Europe, there are many of these central organizations, three of the larger being The British Library Document Supply Center, The Technical Information Library at the University of Hannover in West Germany and the Swiss Institute of Technology in Zurich. The British Library serves the technical needs of the United Kingdom and makes its services available to other European countries.

This same operation would be indispensable in the United States. With conference literature representing a leading source of research information, it is now more vital than ever that a centralized source be developed to house, index, disseminate and expand on this technical knowledge.

APPENDIX 1

1. *Video register & teleconferencing resources directory*. Boston, MA: G.K. Hall; 1988.
2. *The business of nonbroadcast television, corporate & institutional video budgets, facilities and applications*. Boston, MA: G.K. Hall; 1988.
3. *Encyclopedia of associations*. Detroit, MI: Gale Research Co; 1987.
4. *Japan directory of professional associations*. Tokyo, Japan: Japan Publications Guide Service; 1984.
5. *China directory*. Tokyo, Japan: Radiopress Inc; 1986.
6. *Directory of associations in Canada*. Toronto, Ont. Micromedia Ltd.; 1985.
7. *AsLib directory of information sources in the U.K.* London, U.K.: AsLib; 1984.
8. *Directory of European industrial & trade associations*. Beckenham, U.K.: CBD Research Ltd.; 1986.
9. *Centres Francais de documentation scientifique et technique*. Paris, France: A.N.R.T; 1970.
10. *Trade associations and professional bodies of the United Kingdom*. Oxford, U.K.: Pergamon Press; 1985.
11. *Pan European associations*. Beckenham, U.K.: CBD Research Ltd.; 1983.

APPENDIX 2

1988
1987 Initiated development work leading to eventual on-line service
1986
1985
1984 Commenced publication of the Meetings Index
1983
1982
1981
1980
1979
1978
1977
1976
1975
1974 Commenced publication of the Series PCE
1973
1972 published 1st 4 Year Cumulated Volume, Series SSH
1971 published 1st 5 Year Index, Series EEMT
1970
1969
1968 Commenced the Series SSH and designated the basic DIRECTORY Series SEMT
1967
1966
1965 Initiated publication of the DIRECTORY of PUBLISHED PROCEEDINGS
1964 Organized InterDok

Conference Proceedings at the Engineering Societies Library

Kirk Cabeen

SUMMARY. Summarizes the importance of conference papers and proceedings of meetings to the Engineering Societies Library then describes types of papers of primary interest to that library. Also discusses the cataloging and lending techniques involving this sort of material.

ROLE OF CONFERENCE LITERATURE

It should be patently obvious to the librarian or other information specialist who has worked in any field of science and/or technology that conference proceedings represent the cutting edge of what's new. A bright young (maybe not so young) scientist or engineer discovers something, invents something, develops a new process, or improves an existing technique, and, of course, he or she wants the world to know that a genius has burst on the scene. What better way to announce the new discovery than to present a paper at a conference or technical meeting? I do not mean to sound flippant about this practice. It is indeed a valid, perhaps the most valid, way of airing newly acquired knowledge to one's confreres. Of course the necessary clearances from higher-ups in the employee's organization must be obtained before the information may be publicly disseminated, and sometimes patents must be procured prior to a disclosure. Neither of these, however, is the concern of the librarian

---

Kirk Cabeen, until his recent retirement, was Director, Engineering Societies Library, 345 E. 47th St., New York, NY 10017. He received the BS degree (Chemistry) from Lafayette College and the MSLS degree from Syracuse University.

© 1989 by The Haworth Press, Inc. All rights reserved.

whose client learns of the existence of the presentation and wants to read the paper.

The client may have learned about this presentation in a variety of ways: actual attendance at the conference; through a literature search; by word of mouth; or through a reference in the bibliography of another article. In whatever manner he/she (I'm going to be chauvinistic from here on) learns about the paper, he wants it and generally he wants it now or sooner. Unless he picked up a copy of preprinted proceedings at the conference (and didn't turn it over to the company librarian as he should have done) he will probably turn to that company librarian for a copy of the wanted paper. Papers appear in a variety of ways. Some are issued only as reprints, some first as preprints and later printed in a journal, transactions, or proceedings. This latter is true of many professional society papers, at least in the field of engineering.

PROCEDURES AT ESL

All papers presented at the many meetings of the American Society of Mechanical Engineers (ASME) are first issued and given a control number as individual papers. Selectively, many of these are subsequently published in issues of the *ASME Transactions*. Keeping track of which papers were or were not published can be a chore. Because the Engineering Societies Library (ESL) is *the* library for ASME, as well as other engineering societies, we feel it is important to maintain a record of this kind of information. Consequently, as *ASME Transactions* are published, our catalog department carefully checks each article, and notes on a 3 × 5 card which ASME papers (by number) have been published in which issue of the *Transactions*. After two years the published papers are discarded from the individual file. The rest are bound and kept as *ASME Miscellaneous Papers*. The index allows us to access the paper either by the original number, or a citation to the *Transactions*. The Engineering Societies Library also maintains indexes of varying degrees of sophistication to the papers from the Institute of Electrical and Electronic Engineers, the Metallurgical Society, the Society of Automotive Engineers, and the Society of Mining Engineers.

Conference proceedings are frequently published as a regular (or sometimes special) issue of a periodical. When this happens we file the proceedings as part of the periodical, adding a card to our public card catalog under the title of the conference and citing the specific issue of the periodical. Occasionally proceedings may be spread over several issues, and when this happens it is indicated on the card.

At ESL we catalog conference proceedings either under the sponsor of the conference or the exact title. This works fine for the public and official card catalogs, but frequently requesters don't know the sponsor and have a vague or inexact title for the conference. To help alleviate this problem our acquisitions department maintains what we call "The conference file." This is a 3 × 5 card listing filed alphabetically by the first "significant" word in the title. This file has proved to be invaluable to the reference department. The card is originated when the acquisitions department first learns of the existence (either past or future) of the conference. Thereafter or thereon the following information is added when known: who sponsored it; who published proceedings, if published; if it will not be published; if it appeared in a journal, which and what issue(s); when we ordered it; when we received it; the price we paid for it; and the form in which it appeared. Not every card has all this information on it, of course, but as occasionally happens, the fact that no preprints or proceedings have or will be published can save a reference librarian a great deal of time in searching for something that doesn't exist.

Because proceedings papers are in great demand, particularly in the first five years of their existence, the ESL will not lend conference proceedings or individual papers to anyone. When we receive a request for the loan of a volume of proceedings, we send instead a copy of the title page and table of contents with a message that we can supply copies of individual papers.

The conference paper and the conference proceedings are an essential source of information to the scientist and engineer. The procurement and handling of them has been and will continue to be a great problem for librarians and information specialists. In this brief article I have attempted to explain how the staff at the Engineering Societies Library copes with these difficulties.

Conference Proceedings: A Tutorial Module

Nestor L. Osorio

SUMMARY. A tutorial module for learning about conference literature is presented. This module is intended for the use of new science librarians, library assistants, advanced students, faculty members and technical staff who need to verify and identify conference proceedings. The module has three basic components: Summary Sheets of indexing journals and databases; Questions; and a Work Sheet. Questions are recorded on the Work Sheet. To select the appropriate database or index the Work Sheet is compared to the Summary Sheets. Some recommendations about recording the results obtained are presented.

INTRODUCTION

The importance of conference proceedings in the scientific and engineering fields is well described in the literature. J. C. Rowley[1] in a 1980 article said:

> Technical and scientific conferences are organized primarily to present current status and progress reports on a specific subject. They also provide a forum for personal discussion and interactions between conference attendees.

Nestor L. Osorio is Assistant Professor and Science-Engineering Subject Specialist at Northern Illinois University, DeKalb, IL 60115-2868. He holds both the MA (Physics) and the MLS degree from the State University of New York at Geneseo.

This paper is a revised version of a presentation given at the Annual Meeting of the American Society for Engineering Education, Poster Session of the Engineering Libraries Division in Reno, NV, on June 24, 1987.

© 1989 by The Haworth Press, Inc. All rights reserved.

G. Hellyer[2], adding to the increased importance of this segment of the literature stated that:

> Conference, symposia, and seminar are a great way to deal with the information explosion. Meetings permit an easy, timely flow and exchange of information.

Both authors Rowley and Hillyer were participants at the "Workshop on Conference Literature in Science and Technology" that took place in 1980. The Proceedings[3] of this workshop should be recommended as standard reading for librarians in the science and technological fields.

In 1972 D. M. Short[4] estimated that at least ten thousand conferences took place at that time every year and in all disciplines. We can assume that in more recent years this number has increased. The Institute of Scientific Information[5] estimates that for 1988 ten thousand scientific and technical meetings alone have taken place.

It is also well recognized by library users and librarians that conference literature are a source of many bibliographic difficulties. The lack of standardization can be understood by the range of terms that is used to describe a scientific or technical meeting. It can be called among other names: conference, convention, colloquium, congress, discussion, institute, meeting, seminar, session, symposium, summer school, or workshop.

The difficulties of verification in conference literature is described by J. P. Chillag[6] of the British Library Lending Division:

> Conference proceedings are an increasingly numerous and important form of communication. It is, however, notoriously difficult to identify published conference proceedings because they can be referred to in different ways, which rarely conform to those used in standard bibliographic tools.

In an article about identification and verification of conference publications M. M. K. Hlava[7] examined several obstacles usually found when dealing with proceedings: (1) citations are usually incomplete, (2) citations are published with acronyms, (3) names of corporate sources change frequently, (4) conferences are sponsored by multiple corporate sources, (5) conference titles change frequently, (6) conference titles are usually very long.

Another problem is the fact that proceedings are published in several different physical forms. For this reason P. R. Mills[8] divides them into four groups: (1) proceedings that are part of a journal, (2) proceedings that are published as a monograph, with a distinct title, (3) proceedings published as part of a series, and (4) proceedings published as technical reports.

In most cases, library users and science and engineering librarians encounter several problems with this type of literature, they can be summarized as: (1) problems of verification, (2) indexing and abstracting is not always available, (3) some proceedings are never published, and (4) some proceedings are published late.

In more recent years new indexing and abstracting journals have become available, and the use of on-line databases has certainly improved the accessibility of conference proceedings.

Objective

The main objective of this paper is to create a module that can be used as an instructional or tutorial tool for the identification and verification of conference proceedings. It is intended for new librarians in the technical and scientific fields or for library assistants in technical libraries. It can be used also to introduce the bibliographic tools available for this important segment of the literature to advanced students, faculty members or technical staff.

For this purpose six printed bibliographic sources and eight databases will be identified. Printed listings for conference publications are numerous, the ones chosen for this module are considered basic reference tools and it is most likely that at least two of them would be found in any technical or scientific library. Databases are also available in very large numbers and some of them are quite specialized. For the purpose of this module eight are presented as examples of databases that cover conference literature. They were selected because of their significance as comprehensive research sources.

BIBLIOGRAPHIC DESCRIPTION

Print Formats

Six basic indexing journals of conference proceedings publications are selected for this module: *Directory of Published Proceedings, SEMT; Proceedings in Print; World Meetings: United States and Canada; Index to Scientific and Technical Proceedings; Bibliographic Guide to Conference Publications; and Conference Paper Index.*

Summary Sheet 1 serves to identify access points to each of these indexes, it also gives their coverage according to physical formats (see Table 1). Summary Sheet 2 provides information of the elements found in a bibliographic record for each of these six indexes (see Table 2). The section on "Printed Indexes—Description" gives a brief statement of some of the most relevant elements of each source.

Printed Indexes—Description

Directory of Published Proceedings: Series SEMT—Science/Engineering/Medicine/Technology. Harrison, NY: InterDok Corp.; 1965+. Ten issues per year, annual cumulation. It indexes conferences in chronological order by month and year; cites preprints and published proceedings publications such as books, reports, series and journals. It does not index individual papers. In 1986, 3,669 meetings were listed.

Proceedings in Print. Arlington, MA: Proceedings in Print, Inc.; 1964+. Biomonthly, annual cumulation. It is a multidisciplinary index to conference proceedings available in print; covered books, series, reports and journals. In 1986, 3,047 proceedings were listed. It does not index individual papers.

World Meetings: United States and Canada. New York: Macmillan Publishing Company; 1968+. Quarterly. This is an index of forthcoming pure sciences, applied sciences, medical and engineering meetings listed up to two years in advance. It does not index individual papers. *World Meetings: Outside U.S. and Canada* covers meetings in the rest of the world.

Index to Scientific and Technical Proceedings. Philadelphia: Insti-

TABLE 1. Summary Sheet 1: Printed Indexes

Access Points	ISTP	CPI	WM	PIP	DPP/ SEMT	BG CP
Category Index/Subject Headings	X	X		X	X	X
Contents of Proceedings	X	X				
Author/Editor Index	X	X		X	X	X
Sponsor Index	X		X	X	X	X
Subject Index-Keyword Index	X	X	X			
Corporate Index	X			X	X	X
Conference Title Index		X				X
Conference Date Index		X	X		X	
Conference Location Index	X	X	X		X	
Deadline Index			X			
Coverage:						
Proceedings in Journals	X	X	X	X	X	
Proceeding in Book and Series	X	X	X	X	X	X
Papers of Proceedings	X	X				
Unpublished Proceedings		X	X			
Forthcoming Proceedings			X			
Frequency of Publication	M	7/yr	Q	BM	10/yr	A
No. of Conferences Cited, 1986	3,956	220	-	3,047	3,660	-

tute of Scientific Information; 1978+. Monthly, annual cumulation. *ISTP* covers proceedings published in books, reports, series, and journals. It indexes proceedings publications and individual papers. The Permuterm subject index provides multiple access points for searching. Close to 4,000 proceedings were included in 1986.

Bibliographic Guide to Conference Publications. Boston, MA: G. K. Hall Co.; 1975+. Annual. It includes conference proceedings

TABLE 2. Summary Sheet 2: Printed Indexes

Bibliographic Record	ISTP	CPI	WM	PIP	DPP/SEMT	BG/CP
Accession Number	X	X		X	X	
Author/Editor	X	X		X	X	X
Title	X	X		X	X	X
Corp. Source/Author Affiliation	X	X		X		
Conference/Meeting Number						
World Meeting Registry No.		X	X			
Conference Title	X	X	X	X	X	X
Conference Location	X	X	X	X	X	X
Conference Date	X	X	X	X	X	X
Sponsor	X	X	X	X	X	X
Ordering Info./Publisher	X	X	X	X	X	
Source Publication	X	X	X	X	X	
LC Card	X				X	X
ISSN/ISBN	X				X	X
Price	X			X	X	
Journal/Series Title	X		X	X	X	X
Language			X			
Publication Year	X			X	X	X
Report Number	X			X	X	
Keywords/Descriptors					X	X

in all subject fields. This bibliography provides complete LC cataloging information. The list of entries in alphabetical order includes titles, authors, subject headings, and corporate entries. This index represents the conference publications recently cataloged by the New York Public Library and the Library of Congress. It does not index individual paper or proceedings in journals.

Conference Papers Index. Bethesda, MD: Cambridge Scientific Abstracts; 1973+. Seven times per year, annual cumulation. It covers conference publications in scientific, technical, engineering, and medical fields. It includes published and unpublished papers, provides ordering information for acquisition of papers prior to their publication. Also includes books, journals, series, and reports. Cites individual papers. In 1986, about 220 conference proceedings were listed. It covers major national and international conferences.

Databases

Eight databases are included in this section; six of them are databases exclusively devoted to conference literature. The other two, INSPEC and ISMEC, are examples of scientific and technical databases that cover conference proceedings.

Summary Sheet 3 provides information of systems where these files can be retrieved (see Table 3). Summary Sheet 4 lists access points that can be utilized for the verification and identification of conference proceedings when searching these databases (see Table 4). The description part of the databases gives brief information about each file.

Databases – Description

The information in Summary Sheet 3 and in this section was obtained in part from the *Directory of Online Databases*.[9]

INSPEC. Herts, England: Institution of Electrical Engineers; 1969- . Covered Computer Science; engineering; library and information science; physics. 2.7 million citations. Monthly update of 16,000 records. Equivalent printed format: *Science Abstracts: A, B, C, and D*.

ISMEC. Bethesda, MD: Cambridge Scientific Abstracts; 1973- . Covered mechanical engineering, production and engineering management. 176,000 citations. Monthly update of 1,300 records. Equivalent printed format: *ISMEC Bulletin*.

Ei Engineering Meetings. New York, NY: Engineering Informa-

TABLE 3. Summary Sheet 3: Databases

Databases		DIALOG	BRS	ORBIT	STN
Conference Papers Index (CPI)		77			
Ei Engineering Meetings (EiME)		165		EiMET	MEET
INSPEC	(INSP)	12, 13	INSP, INSB	INSPEC	INSPEC
ISMEC	(ISM)	14			
CONF	(CONF)				CONF
CONFERENCE PROCEEDINGS INDEX (BLAISE-LINE)	(CP)				
ISI/ISTP & B (DIMDI)	(ISTP)				
MEETING AGENDA (Telesystems-Questel)	(MAG)				

BLAISE-LINE (The British Library, London, England)

BRS Information Technologies (Latham, NY)

DIALOG Information Services, Inc. (Palo Alto, CA)

DIMDI (Cologne, FRG)

ORBIT Information Technologies Corporation (McLean, VA)

STN International (Chemical Abstracts Service, Columbus, OH)

Telesystems-Questel (Paris, France)

tion, Inc., 1982-1987. Covered engineering and technical meetings. 380,000 citations. Monthly update of 9,000 records, 2,000 proceedings per year.

ISI/ISTP and B. Philadelphia, PA: Institute of Scientific Information; 1978- . Covered all scientific, medical and technical fields. 1.2 million citations. Monthly update of 12,500 records, 3,400 proceedings per year. Equivalent printed format: *Index to Scientific and Technical Proceedings*.

Conference Papers Index. Bethesda, MD: Cambridge Scientific

TABLE 4. Summary Sheet 4: Databases

Access Points	EiME	CPI	INSP	ISM	CONF	ISTP	MAG	CP
System Accession No.	X	X	X	X	X	X		X
Journal Accession No.	X	X	X	X				
Title	X	X	X	X		X		X
Author	X	X	X	X		X		X
Corp. Source/Author Affl.	X	X	X	X		X		X
Conf. Title	X	X	X	X	X	X	X	X
Conf. Location	X	X	X	X	X	X	X	
Conf. Year	X	X	X	X		X		
Conf. Date	X				X	X	X	X
Sponsor	X	X	X	X	X	X	X	
Publisher	X	X	X	X		X		X
Coden	X		X	X				
ISSN, ISBN	X		X	X		X		X
Publication Year	X		X	X		X		X
Conf./Meeting No.		X				X		
Language	X		X	X		X		X
Report No.	X		X	X				
Document Type			X			X		X
Book/Jour./Ser. Title	X		X	X		X		X
Abstract	X		X	X			X	
Descriptors	X	X	X	X	X			X
Identifiers	X	X	X					
Class. Codes/Headings	X	X	X	X	X	X	X	X
Update Frequency (thou.)	9 M	3 M	16 M	1.3 M	.1 W	12.5 M	7.5 Y	1 M

Abstracts; 1973- . Covered all scientific, medical and technical fields. 1 million citations. Monthly update of 3,000 records. Equivalent printed format: *Conference Papers Index*.

CONF. Eggenstein Leopolshafen, FRG: Fachinformationszentrum Energy, Physik, Mathematk GmbH; 1976- . Covered mathematics, physics, engineering and computer science. 40,000 citations. Weekly update of 100 meetings. Does not index individual papers.

Conference Proceedings Index. London, England: The British Library; 1964- . Covered all subject areas with a major emphasis on the sciences. 200,000 citations. Monthly update of 1,000 meetings. Does not index individual papers. Equivalent printed format: *Index of Conference Proceedings Received*.

Meeting Agenda. Cedex, France: Commissariat a L'Energie Atomique (CEA). Centre d'Etudes Nucleaires de Saclay. Covered all scientific and technical fields and social sciences. Announced forthcoming meetings up to 3 years in advance. 15,000 citations per year. Updated twice a month. Does not index individual papers.

Note: OCLC can be a useful database for locating conference materials. An article written by J. N. Hinter[10] described searching techniques for this database.

METHODOLOGY

It was stated in the "Objectives" section of this module that its main purpose is to develop a tutorial unit that can be used for learning about verification and identification of conference proceedings. In order to achieve this objective it is necessary to simulate the conditions that are usually present when conference proceedings are cited in the literature or are verbally requested of a library specialist.

Three basic elements are part of this module: Summary Sheets; Questions; and a Work Sheet. Summary Sheets are presented in the previous section, a Work Sheet is at the end of this section.

Bibliographic Citations and Questions

Bibliographic citations should be gathered from several sources: from bibliographies in books, from indexing journals and from publishers' catalogs. A total of fifty questions is recommended for this module. This number of questions would provide the reader with a variety of simulations that are required to become familiar with the resources used and with the conference literature.

Bibliographic citations identified should be of five kinds: (1) books, including monographic series and reports, (2) articles in books, (3) issues of journals, (4) articles in journals, (5) abstracts of papers published in digest publications.

Questions should be made based on selected information taken from each of the bibliographic records. Thus, the complete information about the meeting or the paper should never be given. The following are five examples of questions and its corresponding bibliographic records.

Type 1 Question. Books, including monographic series and reports.
*Question:*Title of the proceeding: Factory of the Future. Proceedings of the 8th Conference on Production Research. Approximate conference date: 1984 or 1985.

Bibliographic record. Toward the Factory of the Future. Proceedings of the 8th International Conference on Production Research and the 5th Working Conference of the Fraunhofer Inst. for Industrial Engineering (FHG-IAO), Stuttgart, 1985. Editors: Bullinger, H. J. and H. J. Warnecke. Springer-Verlag; New York; 1985. $120.00. ISBN 0-387-15762-X.

Type 2 Question. Articles in books.
Question: Article about Digital Simulation, by John P. Hayes from the Dept. of Elect. Eng., Univ. of Michigan; Ann Arbor, presented at ICCD '84.

Bibliographic record. A Systematic Approach to Multivalued Digital Simulation. John P. Hayes (Dept. of Elect. Eng. and Comp. Sci., Univ. of Michigan; Ann Arbor). Proceedings IEEE International Conference on Computer Design: VLSI in Computers. Sponsored by IEEE Computer Society and IEEE Circuits and Systems

Society. ICCD '84. Port Chester, New York, October 8-11, 1984. ISBN 0-8186-0563-8. LC 84-81843. IEEE Computer Society Press, 1984. p. 177-182.

Type 3 Question. Issues of journals.
Question: Title of the Journal: IEE Journal of Quantum Electronics. Papers of the 8th Semiconductor Laser Conference. The meeting took place in the last five years.

Bibliographic record. Semiconductor Laser Conference, 8th IEEE International held Sept. 13-15, 1982 in Ottawa, Ontario, Canada; sponsored by IEEE QEA. Papers in IEEE Journal of Quantum Electronics, vol. QE-19, No. 6, June 1983, 199 pp., $18.00.

Type 4 Question. Articles in journals.
Question: Paper presented by S. S. Chen of Argonne Natl. Lab., in SMiRT-7, the 7th International Conference of Structural mechanics.

Bibliographic record. Stability of Tube Arrays in Crossflow. Chen, S. S. (Argonne Natl. Lab., Components Technology Div., Argonne, IL, USA); and Jendrzejcyk, J. A. Nucl. Eng. Des. v. 75, n. 3, Jun. 1983. SMiRT-7, 7th Int. Conf. on Structural Mech. in React. Technol. Chicago, IL, USA, Aug. 22-26, 1983. p. 351-373.

Type 5 Question. Abstracts of papers in digest publications.
Question: Abstract about a survey on medical lasers by two people from the Massachusetts General Hospital, presented at CLEO '85.

Bibliographic record. New medical users of lasers: a survey. Thomas F. Deutsch and Allan R. Oseroff (Massachusetts General Hospital, Wellman Laboratory, Mass.). In: Conference on Lasers and Electro-Optics, 21-24 May 1985. CLEO '85. OSA/IEEE. Baltimore, Maryland. Digest of Technical Papers. Optical Society of America/IEEE, 1985. LC 85-60920.

The next step is to develop a Work Sheet. The purpose of this sheet is to record the vital information given in each question.

Summary Sheets 1, 2 and 4 provide the reader with the characteristics and access points of indexes and databases. The Work Sheet will be used to compare the information obtained from each question with the information presented in the Summary Sheets about the databases and the indexing journals. The next step is to select the appropriate printed index or database that would be used for verification and identification of the meeting or paper.

Figure 1 is a schematic representation of the process. The five examples of questions are tabulated in the Work Sheet sample (see Table 5).

RESULTS

Results of each tutorial session should be tabulated. In this section a Tabulation Form is presented (see Table 6). It is important to remember that the level of difficulty of the questions should be made so as to resemble similar situations found when dealing with conference proceedings. The results obtained in a tutorial session are then directly related to the information given in each question. Therefore, this exercise is not intended to be a technique for evaluating indexing journals or databases used, but aims at making the reader familiar with these bibliographic resources. By working with them the trainee will discover that each of them has a well defined purpose.

In Table 6 the scale 0, 1, 2 represents the number of years from the time the meeting was held to the time it appeared indexed.

Another result that can be recorded is the number of times an answer to a question was found in the indexes or databases used. It could be presented in this form:

	No. of questions
Not found	/
Found in One Index/Database	/
Found in Two Indexes/Databases	/
Found in Three Indexes/Databases	/
Found in Four Indexes/Databases	/
Found in Five Indexes	/

Questions are searched in indexing journals or databases according to the information given and to the characteristic of each source; therefore, not all questions are searchable in all indexes or databases.

TABLE 5. Work Sheet

	T1	T2	T3	T4	T5
Book (Include monographic series)	X				
Article in a Book		X			
Issue of a Journal			X		
Article in a Journal				X	
Abstract from a Digest					X
Title	P	P		X	P
Author/Editor		X		X	
Corp. Source/Author Affil.		X		X	X
Conference Title	P	P	X	P	P
Conference Location					
Conference Year	A	X			X
Conference Date					
Sponsor					
Source Publication					
Publisher					
Coden (Journal)					
ISSN; ISBN					
Publication Year					
Conference/Meeting Number					
Language					
Report Number					
Journal/Series Title			X		
Subject Terms	X	X	X		X
Class Codes					

P=partial   A=approx.

```
                                      +----------+
                               +->| Summary  +-> Printed
+-------------+   +----------+ |  | Sheet 1  |    Source
| Questions   |   | Working  +--+ +----------+
| 1.        +-->| Sheet      +--+ +----------+
| 2.          |   |          |  +->| Summary  +-> Database
                               |  | Sheet 2  |
                                  +----------+
```

Figure 1

TABLE 6. Tabulation Form

	Indexes					Databases			
	PIP	SEMT	BHCP	ISTP	CPI	E1EM	INSP	ISMEC	CPI
No. of Searches									
No. Found									
% Found									
Time in Minutes									
Ave. Time/ Search									
Scale: 0									
1									
2									

REFERENCES

1. Rowley, John C. The conference literature—savory or acrid? *In:* Zamora, Gloria J.; Adamson, Martha C., eds. *Conference literature: its role in the distribution of information; proceedings of the workshop on conference literature in science and technology.* 1980 May 1-3. Marlton, NJ: Learned Information; 1981: p. 11-21.

2. Hillyer, Georgiana. Announcements of forthcoming meetings. *In:* Zamora, Gloria J.; Adamson, Martha C., eds. *Conference literature: its role in the*

distribution of information; proceedings of the workshop on conference literature in science and technology. 1980 May 1-3, Marlton, NJ: Learned Information; 1981: p. 44-52.

3. Zamora, Gloria J.; Adamson, Martha C., eds. *Conference literature: its role in the distribution of information; proceedings of the workshop on conference literature in science and technology.* 1980 May 1-3. Marlton, NJ: Learned Information; 1981. 220p.

4. Short, P.J. Bibliographic tools for tracing conference proceedings. *IATUL Proceedings.* 2(2): 50-53; 1972 May.

5. Statistical summary. *Index to Scientific and Technical Proceedings.* (8):xvii; 1986 August.

6. Chillag, John P. 120,000 conference proceedings from stock: the conference collection and database at the British Library Lending Division. *In*: Zamora, Gloria J.; Adamson, Martha C., eds. *Conference literature: its role in the distribution of information; proceedings of the workshop on conference literature in science and technology.* 1980 May 1-3. Marlton, NJ: Learned Information; 1981: p. 148-157.

7. Hlava, Marjorie M.K. Online identification, verification and ordering of conference publications. *In*: Zamora, Gloria J.; Adamson, Martha C., eds. *Conference literature: its role in the distribution of information; proceedings of the workshop on conference literature in science and technology.* 1980 May 1-3. Marlton, NJ: Learned Information; 1981: p. 166-179.

8. Mills, P.R. Characteristic of published conference proceedings. *Journal of Documentation.* 29(1): 36-50; 1973 March.

9. *Directory of Online Databases.* 8(1); 1987 January, New York: Cuadra/Elsevier.

10. Hintner, Jo Nell. Cataloging, and finding, conference publications using OCLC. *In*: Zamora, Gloria J.; Adamson, Martha C., eds. *Conference literature: its role in the distribution of information; proceedings of the workshop on conference literature in science and technology.* 1980 May 1-3. Marlton, NJ: Learned Information; 1981: p. 192-202.

APPENDIX

This appendix includes a partial list of journals; indexes and abstracts; and reference sources that can be useful for the verification and identification of conference literature.

Journals

American Nuclear Society Transactions
Astronautics and Aeronautics
The Bulletin of the American Physical Society
Chemical and Engineering News

Chemical Engineering Progress
Chemistry and Industry
Europhysics News
IEEE Spectrum
International Chemical Engineering
Journal of the Optical Society of America
Journal of the Electrochemical Society
Laser Focus
Microprocessors and Microsystems
Mechanical Engineering
Nature
Nuclear News
Physics Today
Science
Simulation

Indexes and Abstracts

Bibliography and Index of Geology
Biological Abstracts
Chemical Abstracts
Current Programs
Energy Research Abstracts
Engineering Index
Ergonomics Abstracts
IEEE Technical Activities Guide
Index Medicus
Index of Conference Proceedings Received
Index to IEEE Publications
International Aerospace Abstracts
ISMEC Bulletin
Mathematical Reviews
Metals Abstracts
Nuclear Science Abstracts
Science Abstracts A, B, C and D
Scientific and Technical Aerospace Reports

Reference Sources

American Men and Women of Science
Books in Print
CASSI: Chemical Abstracts Service Source Index
Directory of American Research and Technology

Encyclopedia of Associations
European Research Index
Irregular Serials and Annuals
National Faculty Directory
National Union Catalog
New Serial Titles and Supplements
Publishers International Directory
Ulrich's International Periodicals Directory
Who's Who in Technology Today

SCI-TECH COLLECTIONS

Tony Stankus, Editor

Generating sustained interest and support from nonscientists for astronomical and astrophysical research can be difficult. In part this is because most people tend to think of the night sky as essentially unchanging. Of course the assortment of visible planets and constellations changes with the seasons, but each season's view is fairly constant from year to year. Fortunately, from time to time, the finer changes noted by experts do get popular press. Every few years, photos from space probes of closer planetary detail stir some interest, as do announcements of ever more distant stars discovered from more powerful earth telescopes. Likewise the reappearance of a comet at decades-long intervals, prompts a revival of popular support out of a mixture of fear and wonder. But something that has been detected only a few times in recorded human history was noted in February 1987. A star essentially "detonated" into a supernova. A number of popular accounts have appeared and a renaissance of supernova thinking is underway. We are fortunate to have the much credentialled David Stern, an active member of the Physics-Astronomy-Mathematics section of SLA, and contributor to *Special Libraries*, provide us with a librarian's guide.

I once again urge busy sci-tech librarians to submit subject survey/subject collection papers. Advances in your field of interest may well help the larger sci-tech library community serve its clientele better.

Supernovae: A Guide to the Literature

David Stern

WHAT IS A SUPERNOVA?

A supernova is the explosion of a large, late-stage star. There are different types of supernovae, but the great majority fall into Type I or Type II. Type I supernovae are believed to originate from a pair of stars, the progenitor star (the star before it exploded into what was seen as the supernova) being an old star (a white dwarf) that attracts and burns the hydrogen gas of a nearby younger star (this process is known as accretion). The white dwarf begins by burning hydrogen into helium, then helium into carbon and oxygen. Eventually the white dwarf mass grows beyond the stable Chandrasekhar limit of 1.4 solar masses, and the carbon in the star's core ignites, creating the explosion that is the supernova.

Type II supernovae originate from a supergiant (beyond main-stage) star of greater than eight solar masses, with a diameter of about 10 astronomical units (the distance from the earth to the sun). When the star's source of available hydrogen gets very low, the temperature of the star starts to increase and the star expands to 50 times its original size. This red giant then begins to undergo thermonuclear fusion and forms heavier elements in the core of the star. Eventually neutrinos are produced and emitted, carrying away energy and outward pressure. Gravity, now unopposed, causes the star to contract. The star collapses in upon itself, creating tremen-

---

David Stern holds degrees in Biology (U. Conn.), the History and Philosophy of Science, and Library and Information Science (both Indiana U.). He is currently Physics/Astronomy Librarian and Assistant Professor of Library Administration at the University of Illinois at Urbana-Champaign, Urbana, IL 61801.

dous pressure and heat as the atomic particles are jammed into a very small space. (The star which started at approximately 20 times the size of our sun has been concentrated into a dense ball of atomic material the size of the earth—109 times smaller than the sun.) This unstable situation results in a thermonuclear explosion which blows off most of the star's material into space at high velocity. This explosion results in a bright flash of light in the optical wavelengths (those visible to the naked eye or the lens-aided eye of an optical telescope) that registers over an absolute magnitude of -15 (100 times more luminous than an ordinary nova, a simple explosion of a smaller star). Energy is also released in the other wavelengths (ultraviolet, x-ray, gamma ray) that are not visible to the naked eye, but which can be detected by other types of telescopes or receivers. The energy released during this explosion is equal to the energy released by our sun over nine billion years. Supernovae are the largest energy-releasing events ever witnessed by man; they are second only to the Big Bang at the start of the universe in terms of total energy release.

The results of this explosion are (1) a shell of gaseous debris which expands outward and is known as a supernova remnant (these objects are optically faint, but strong emitters of radio and x-rays) and (2) occasionally, a remainder of the original star's core as a compact object (a neutron star, a pulsar, or a black hole) depending upon the mass of the original progenitor star.

There are more than 400 identified supernovae from outside our Milky Way galaxy. In addition, there have been supernovae recorded in our galaxy, the most famous being Tycho's star of 1572, Kepler's star of 1604, and a Chinese observation in 1054 which was believed to be the progenitor of the famous Crab Nebula. Cassiopeia A is a very strongly emitting supernova remnant that exploded approximately 300 years ago, but was not detected at that time. It is predicted that there are approximately two or three supernovae per century in our galaxy.

RECENT ACTIVITY

A great opportunity for studying supernovae occurred on February 23, 1987. What had been primarily a theoretical field dependent upon archival studies and model development became an observational field as there was a nearby supernova in the Large Magellanic Cloud, a small neighboring galaxy visible from the Southern Hemisphere. This event (which occurred approximately 170,000 years ago, and whose light has just reached us through the enormous distances of space) known as SN 1987a (the first observed supernova of 1987) was believed to be the supernova explosion of a star known as Sanduleak − 69 202 (the numbers relate to its position in the sky according to a grid system very similar to longitude and latitude as found on terrestrial maps). The discovery was quickly announced via telephone, telegraph, and computer networks, and the observing instruments of the entire world were focused upon the new astronomical occurrence. Never before has there been the opportunity to study a supernova under such ideal conditions, and with the latest available technology.

IMPORTANCE OF THE NEW OBSERVATIONS

The data are just starting to be analysed, but already there has been great confusion and excitement for the entire astronomical community. Theories are being continually revised, disproved, and advanced. As more data come in within the next few years, there will be great implications for all of the physical sciences. Questions in areas such as fundamental particle physics (neutrino production and mass), cosmology (stellar and galactic evolution, heavy element production and dissemination, the closed vs. open nature of the universe in relation to neutrino mass), and astrometry (distance indicators) will be addressed with new empirical data.

Of prime importance at this moment is the question of neutrino production and characteristics. At the present time, calculations show that 85% of the mass of the universe is unaccounted for and exists as some form of "dark matter." Some of this dark matter may be neutrinos left over from the Big Bang. On 07:35 GMT (Greenwich [UK] Mean Time) on February 23, 1987, neutrinos were detected on earth at three underground neutrino detectors. The mass of the neutrinos can be determined by careful calculation of the light emitted as these neutrinos passed through the liquid in the detector tanks. If the mass of the neutrinos is greater than 15 eV, then their total gravitational energy will overcome the observed expansion of the universe, the universe will eventually collapse in upon itself in what is called a "closed" universe scenario. Preliminary calculations give an upper limit of 6-10 eV for the neutrino mass, indicating that the neutrino is probably not massive enough to stop the expansion of the universe without additional dark matter being identified.

IMPACT ON THE LITERATURE

There already exists an historical body of supernova literature, from a worldwide collection of observatory catalogues and research articles in astronomy journals and monographs. Increasing numbers of researchers, at ever-increasing numbers of academic institutions (with the usual publication pressures) produce an increasing body of data and theoretical analyses which are published in the continually expanding number of astronomy journals.

New technology leads to new data, which in turn adds even more to the increasing body of literature.

Additionally, as the supernova gas envelope becomes more transparent over the next decades, more data will flood into the literature, resulting in even greater numbers of analyses and publications.

FINDING THE AVAILABLE RESOURCES

LC Subject Headings

headings beginning with "Supernovae" or "Supernova"
examples: Supernova remnants — congresses
       Supernovae
       Supernovae — congresses
       Supernovae — popular works
       Supernovae — spectra — congresses
       Supernovae as distance indicators — congresses

Library call numbers

Library of Congress: QB841
Dewey Decimal: 523.8446

Books in Print/British Books In Print

Look under subject "supernovae."

Union Catalog(s)

Check local library catalogs under subject/author/title.
Check the *Catalog of the Naval Observatory Library*
   Boston, Mass: G.K. Hall; 1976. 6 volumes.

POPULAR MATERIAL

(* identifies somewhat more technical material, suitable for undergraduate level readers)

Bibliographies

There are excellent astonomy bibliographies listed later in the Research Material section; however, there is a dated and noncomprehensive bibliography geared for the student, layperson or librarian:

Seal, Robert A. *A guide to the literature of astronomy*. Littleton, Colo.: Libraries Unlimited; 1977.

Books

(a sample of the available monographs)

Asimov, Isaac, *The exploding suns: the secrets of the supernovas*. New York:Dutton; 1985. OR New York:New American Library; 1986.
   The first eight chapters discuss supernovae in nontechnical terms while providing a good deal of factual information. The last three chapters discuss the possible impact of supernova debris on the evolutionary process.

*Clark, David H. *The historical supernovae*. New York:Pergamon; 1977.
   An historical perspective from records of the Far East, suitable for interdisciplinary studies in astronomy and the history of science. Chapters 1-4 provide a good overview for beginners, chapter 5-12 contain more advanced material.

Clark, David H. *Superstars: how stellar explosions shape the destiny of our universe*. New York:McGraw-Hill; 1984.
> An informative and entertaining compilation of supernova history and theory.

*Hoffmeister, C. *Variable stars*. New York:Springer-Verlag;1985.
> A translation from the German *Veranderliche sterne* by S. Dunlop. Supernovae discussed within the larger variable star context. Includes an excellent literature review and bibliography.

Mitton, Simon. *The crab nebula*. New York:Scribner; 1978.
> An historical synopsis of the Crab Nebula supernova remnant discoveries.

Murdin, Paul; Murdin, Lesley. *The new astronomy: black holes, white dwarfs, pulsars, and supernovae, how the new astronomy is changing our concepts of the universe*. New York:Crowell; 1978.
> An entertaining look at astronomy's contribution to our view of the universe, by these respected astronomy writers.

*Murdin, Paul; Murdin, Lesley. *Supernova*. Rev. ed. New York:Cambridge University Press; 1985.
> An excellent overview of supernovae, incorporating the latest available information (at that time), by acknowledged leaders in popular astronomy writing.

*Petit, Michel. *Variable stars*. New York:Wiley; 1987.
> A translation from the French *Les etoiles variables* by W.J. Duffin. A chapter on supernovae within the larger topic of variable stars.

*Rowan-Robinson, Michael. *The cosmological distance ladder: distance and time in the universe*. New York:W.H. Freeman; 1985.
> The discussion of a hotly debated topic, in which supernovae play a central role, from a unique perspective.

Straka, W.C. *The supernova: a stellar spectacle*. Washington, D.C.:NASA; 1976. (For sale by the Supt. of Docs., U.S. Govt. Print. Off.);

"A curriculum project of the American Astronomical Society ..." A government document (NAS 1.19:126), a good primer for amateur astronomers or interested laypersons.

*Verschuur, Gerrit L. *The invisible universe; the story of radio astronomy*. New York:Springer-Verlag; 1987.
A completely rewritten version of the 1974 title, a nontechnical (interested-layperson) approach to all of radio astronomy, including supernovae.

Newspapers

The current activity in supernova research leads to the reporting of the latest nontechnical details of SN 1987A in the major American newspapers. Various indexes can be scanned in order to identify the relevant articles, including the *New York Times Index*, the *Washington Post Index*, *Newsbank* which contains microform clippings from major U.S. newspapers, and the most recent indexing available online through commercial vendors such as DIALOG (File 211), BRS (Newsearch and National Newspaper Index), and NEXIS.

Magazines/journals

The major magazines for nontechnical astronomy information are;

Astronomy.
    Milwaukee, WI:Astro Media Corp.
Sky & Telescope.
    Cambridge, MA: Sky Publishing Corp.

They contain informative articles, the latest news, monthly sky charts, and beautiful pictures. (See the special supernova issue of *Astronomy*, February 1988.)

Journals containing more technical articles include *Science News*, *Scientific American*, *Physics Today*, *Nature* (News and Views, Letters sections), and *Science*. Some of these articles may be too technical for beginners.

Indexes to the above mentioned magazines and journals

(as well as other magazines containing popular astronomy articles)

Specific magazine articles can be identified by subject ("supernova" is an acceptable subject heading) in the *Readers Guide to Periodical Literature* and *General Science Index*. This information can also be obtained through these same WILSONLINE databases either online or on CD-ROM.

Electronic news service

Sky & Telescope magazine maintains a bulletin board for late breaking astronomy news that is accessible to computer owners with modems and CompuServe passwords. Once you log on to CompuServe, type GO SKYNEWS at any ! prompt. Then you select the *Sky & Telescope* menu item desired.

Slides/filmstrips

The Astronomical Society of the Pacific (1290 24th Avenue, San Francisco, CA 94122) produces slide sets and accompanying materials for a variety of subjects. AS 295 is the Supernova 1987A set of six slides which sells for $8.

The American Iron and Steel Institute produced a 1984 filmstrip entitled "From supernovas to scientists to you" geared for juvenile audiences which discusses the cosmology and chemistry of our solar system.

RESEARCH MATERIAL

Bibliographies

There are excellent astronomy bibliographies that will lead you to the appropriate citations and catalogs for most topics:

Collins, Mike. *Astronomical catalogues, 1951-1975*. London:Institution of Electrical Engineers; 1977. (INSPEC Bibliography Series; No. 2)
> Pages 129-131 list supernova catalogs found in journals, more recent catalogs are continually updated in the scientific journals.

Kemp, D.A. *Astronomy and astrophysics: a bibliographical guide*. Hamden, CT:Archon Books; 1970.

The original comprehensive sourcebook for the years 1950-1968. Section 57 is the "Novae and Supernovae."

Seal, Robert A.; Martin, Sarah S. *A bibliography of astronomy, 1970-1979*. Littleton, Colo.:Libraries Unlimited; 1982.
Updates the above by Kemp. The definitive bibliography of the years 1969-1978. Should be in all libraries.

Online non-bibliographic databases

A new form of database is the online catalog SIMBAD, a combination bibliographic reference and collection of various astronomical catalogs kept up to date in Strasbourg, France and searchable via international Telenet with the appropriate passwords.

There is an online SN 1987A Bulletin board located at the Space Telescope Science Institute, Baltimore, MD. For more information see the STScI Preprint Series number 223.

The IAU Circulars, an alerting service for observational astronomers, are available both online and on paper from the Central Bureau for Astronomical Telegrams, Smithsonian Astrophysical Observatory, Cambridge, MA 12138.

Monographs

The following is a list of non-conference books on the subject of supernovae:

Aller, Lawrence H.; McLaughlin, Dean B. *Stellar structure*(Stars and Stellar Systems, Vol 8). Chicago:University of Chicago Press; 1965.
Part 6 is "Theory of Novae and Supernovae" and Part 7 is "Supernovae."

Barnes, C.A. et al. *Essays in nuclear astrophysics*: presented to William A. Fowler. Cambridge, England:Cambridge University Press; 1982.
A superb collection of articles by leading researchs in the various fields of nuclear astrophysics, with three articles on supernovae.

Benvenuti, P. *An atlas of UV Spectra of Supernovae* (ESA SP-1046). Paris, France:European Space Agency; 1982.

Clayton, Donald D. *Principles of stellar evolution and nucleosynthesis: with a new preface*. Chicago:University of Chicago Press; 1983.
  An excellent textbook/primer for stellar evolution.

Katz, Jonathan I. *High energy astrophysics* (Frontiers in Physics 63). Menlo Park, CA:Addison-Wesley; 1987.
  A review of the various high-energy phenomena in astrophysics, with a section on supernovae.

Lamb, Frederick K. *High energy astrophysics*. California:Benjamin/Cummings; 1985.
  Reprints from the *Annual Review of Nuclear and Particle Science* and the *Annual Review of Astronomy and Astrophysics* between 1979 and 1984.

Narlikar, Jayant Vishnu. *Violent phenomena in the universe*. Oxford;New York:Oxford University Press; 1982.
  A section of this book deals with supernovae, from both ground-based and air-borne observatories perspectives.

Shklovskii, Iosif S. *Stars: their birth, life, and death*. San Francisco:W.H. Freeman; 1978.
  Revised translation by Richard B. Rodman of the original Russion "Zvezdy, ikh rozhdenie, zhizn i smert." A serious popular book. Includes an excellent bibliography for further reading.

Shklovskii, I.S. *Supernovae*. (Monographs and Texts in Physics and Astronomy Vol. XXI.) New York:Wiley-Interscience; 1968.
  The first attempt (and still a classic) to coordinate the ever-expanding field of supernovae.

Soviet Scientific Reviews: Section E—Astrophysics and Space Physics Reviews
This series is composed of English translations. All volumes have relevant material, especially:
  Vol. 6 "Supernovae Remnants and Their Progenitors."
  Vol. 5 "Thermonuclear Processes in Accreting White Dwarfs (Novae, Symbiotic Stars, and Type-I Supernovae."
  Vol. 3 "Supernovae Remnants: Observational Data. Evolution in the Interstellar Medium."

Book series

Many astronomy monographs are released as part of a series of related books that individual publishers make available on a standing order basis. Examples of important series include: Astrophysics and Space Science Library (Reidel); IAU Highlights, IAU Symposia, IAU Colloquia; Recontre de Moriond (Editions Frontiers); Astronomy and Space Physics Reviews (Sov. Physics Reviews E); Annual Review of Astronomy and Astrophysics; and the NATO Advanced Sciences Institutes (ASI) C: Mathematical and Physical Sciences series (Reidel). See the lists of conferences and monographs for specific relevant titles within these series.

Dissertations

Dissertations in astronomy can be identified using *Dissertations Abstracts International*, Part B, the sciences and engineering. Ann Arbor, MI:University Microfilms International. Annual.

Preprints

Many observatories and academic departments produce preprint series, which are exchanged and serve as prepublication awareness tools.

Organizations

Professional astronomy and astrophysics organizations often hold conferences on specific astronomy topics. These conferences are published as proceedings (see the Conferences section for specific supernova-related publications). Some important organizations include the American Astronomical Society, the British Astronomical Society, the Royal Astronomocial Society of New Zealand, the Royal Astronomical Society (London), the Royal Astronomical Society of Canada, the America Association of Variable Star Observers (AAVSO), the American Physical Society, the International Astronomical Union, the American Institute of Physics, the Astronomical Society of the Pacific, and the Institute of Physics (Great Britain).

Catalog(s)

Green, D.A., *A catalogue of galactic supernova remnants*: last updated 19 March 1987. (SNR Catalogue IV.1) Cambridge:Mullard Radio Astronomy Observatory; 1987.

A very obscure catalogue of supernovae is found in *Acta cosmologica* (Warszawa-Krakow, Poland), Volume 8, 1979.

Flin, Piotr; Karpowicz, Maria; Murawski, Walter; and Rudnicki, Konrad. "Catalogue of Supernovae"
> This catalogue is intended to provide a complete listing of all relevant data on individual supernovae through 1976. There are lists of supernovae, suspected and false supernovae, cluster membership of parent galaxies, checklists, and excellent bibliographies. Lists are arranged by right ascension, Zwicky number, NGC number, Messier number, Henry Draper Catalogue number, BD, CoD, and GC numbers, and according to their physical types (to list a few of the categories).

Conferences

Many scientific meetings, colloquia, etc. are published as proceedings of a conference. This is certainly the case in the area of supernovae. Many of the most important monographs are proceedings of conferences:

Arnett, W.D. *Cosmogonical processes*. Utrecht, Netherlands: VSP; 1986.
> A symposium discussing supernovae among other evolutionary topics (dark matter, galaxies, protoplanets).

Arnett, W.D.; Truran, James W. *Nucleosynthesis: challenges and new developments*. Chicago:University of Chicago Press; 1985.

Audouze, J. et al. *Nucleosynthesis and chemical evolution*(16th Advanced Course of the Swiss Society of Astrophysics and Astronomy, Saas-Fee, March 1986). Sauverny/Versoix, Switzerland:Geneva Observatory; 1987.

Bansel, Daniel; Signore, Monique. *Problems of collapse and numerical relativity* (NATO ASI Series C:134). Boston:Reidel; 1984.

Workshop topic: collapse of iron cores of highly evolved massive stars.

Bartel, Norbert. *Supernovae as distance indicators* (Lecture Notes in Physics 224). New York:Springer-Verlag; 1985.
Discusses methods of distance determination, stressing new accuracy versus other methods.

Brancazio, Peter J; Cameron, A.G.W. *Supernovae and their remnants*. New York: Gordon and Breach; 1969.

Cameron, A.G.W. *Cosmochemistry; proceedings...* (Astrophysics and Space Science Library 40). Boston:Reidel; 1973.
J.W. Truran article on "Theories of nucleosynthesis" includes a section on supernova nucleosynthesis.

Chiosi, Cesare; Renzini, Alvio. *Stellar nucleosynthesis* (Astrophysics and Space Science Library 109). Boston:Reidel; 1984.
Third workshop of the Advanced School of Astronomy of the Ettore Majorana Centre, Erice, Italy (1983). Part I is Planetary Nebulae, Supernovae, Supernovae Remnants and Cosmic Rays; Part IV is Supernovae precursors and explosive nucleosynthesis.

Cosmovici, Crisiano Batalli. *Supernovae and supernova remnants* (Astrophysics and Space Science Library 45). Boston:Reidel; 1974.
An important early conference in Leece, Italy.

Crab Nebula Symposium. *Publications of the Astronomical Society of the Pacific* 82, No. 486 (May 1970), pages 375-564.

Danziger, John. *Proceedings of the ESO Workshop on SN 1987A* (July, 1987). Garching:European Southern Observatory; 1988.

Danziger, John; Gorenstein, Paul. *Supernova remnants and their X-ray emission* (IAU Symposium 101). Boston:Reidel; 1983.
A very important conference containing expert papers on both theoretical and observational supernovae studies.

Giacconi, Ricardo; Setti, Giancarlo. *X-ray astronomy*: proceedings ... (NATO ASI Series C:60). Boston:Reidel; 1980.
Discusses supernovae within the larger topic of x-ray studies.

Gursky, Herbert; Ruffini, Remo. *Neutron stars, black holes, and binary X-ray sources* (Astrophysics and Space Science Library 48). Boston:Reidel; 1978.
   A small section (pp. 13-22) on supernovae, within the larger context of stellar evolution.

Helfand, D.J.; Huang, J.H. *The origin and evolution of neutron stars* (IAU Symposium 125). Boston:Reidel; 1987.
   The latest symposium on neutron stars, with sections on (1) pulsars and supernovae remnants, (2) neutron star physics, and (3) neutron star formation in theoretical supernovae.

Hillebrandt, W. et al. *Nuclear astrophysics* (Lecture Notes in Physics 287). New York:Springer-Verlag; 1987.
   Section III is "Supernovae and SN 1987A."

Hudson, H.S. *High-energy astrophysics* (Advances in Space Research << The Official Journal of the Committee on Space Research (COSPAR)>> Vol. 1, No. 13). Pergamon; 1981.
   Part I "Theoretical Problems in High-energy Astrophysics" has three articles on supernovae.

Kafatos, Minas C.; Henry, Richard B.C. *The crab nebula and related supernova remnants*. Cambridge:Cambridge University Press; 1985.
   A review of astronomical instrumentation and computer modeling as it relates to both the Crab Nebula in detail and supernova remnant theory and observation in general.

Kafatos, Minas C. *Supernova 1987A in the large magellanic cloud*. New York:Cambridge University Press; 1988 (in press).

Kwok, S.; Pottasch, S.R. *Late stages of stellar evolution* (Astrophysics and Space Science Library). Boston:Reidel; 1987.
   Discusses stellar evolution from the optical, infrared, radio, and theoretical perspectives.

Maeder, Andre; Renzini, Alvio. *Observational tests of the stellar evolution theory* (IAU Symposia 105). Boston:Reidel; 1984.
   A related topic which impacts upon theoretical modeling.

Meyerott, Roland; Gillespie, George H. *Supernovae spectra* (American Institute of Physics Conference Proceedings 63), New York: AIP; 1980.

Nomoto, K. *Atmospheric diagnostics of stellar evolution* (IAU Colloquium 108). Boston:Reidel; 1988 (in press).

Novae, Novides et Supernovae. *Colloques Internationaux du Centre National de la Recherche Scientifique* No. 121, 1965. Conference of Saint-Michel de Haute-Provence; 1963 September.

Osborne, J.L.; Wolfendale, A.W. *Origin of cosmic rays* (NATO ASI Series C:14). Boston:Reidel; 1975.
The final four articles are on supernovae.

Pacini, Franco. *High energy phenomena around collapsed stars* (NATO ASI C:195). Boston:Reidel; 1987.
An important collection of lectures from a recent conference covering the broad range of supernova studies.

Pottasch, Stuart R. *Planetary nebulae: a study of late stages of stellar evolution*. Boston:Reidel; 1984.

Pretzl, K. *Low temperature detectors for neutrinos and dark matter*. New York:Springer-Verlag; 1987.

Roger, R.S. *Supernova remnants and the interstellar medium* (IAU Colloquium 101). Cambridge, MA: Cambridge University Press; 1988.

Schramm, David, N. *Supernovae*: the proceedings of a Special IAU Session on Supernovae . . . (Astrophysics and Space Science Library 66). Boston:Reidel; 1977.
Updates earlier ASSL 45, discusses observational and theoretical supernova studies.

Schramm, David N.; Arnett, W. David. *Explosive nucleosynthesis*. Austin:University of Texas Press; 1973.

Sieber, W.; Wielebinski, R. *Pulsars* (IAU Symposium 95). Boston:Reidel; 1981.
Somewhat related material, with a small section on pulsars and supernovae.

Srinivasan, G.; Radhakrishnan, V. *Proceedings of the academy workshop on supernovae, their progenitors and remnants*. (A supplement to *Journal of Astrophysics and Astronomy*.) Bangalore:Indian Academy of Sciences; 1985.

Supernovae and Supernova Remnants. *Memorie della Sociea Astronomica Italiana* 49(2-3); 1978 Aprile-Settembre.
  First workshop of the Advanced School of Astronomy "E. Majorana" Centre for Scientific Culture, Erice-Italy.

Swings, J.P. *Highlights of astronomy (IAU)*, Volume 7. Boston:Reidel; 1986.
  Section 7 "Supernovae" includes a large number of articles.

Tayler, R.J.; Hesser, J.E. *Late stages of stellar evolution* (IAU Symposium No. 66). Boston:Reidel; 1974.
  Copernicus Symposium V.

Texas Symposium on Relativistic Astrophysics

  Ulmer, Melville P., *13th Texas Symposium* . . . , New Jersey:World Scientific; 1987.

Previous Texas Symposia were published in the *Annals of the New York Academy of Sciences*:
  12th, ed. by Livio, Nario and Shaviv, Giora. Vol. 470, 1986, May 30.
  11th, ed. by Evans, David S. Vol. 422; 1984 March 23.
  9th, ed. by Jurgen Ehlers et al. Vol. 336; 1980 Feb 15.
  8th, ed. by Papagiannis, Michael D. Vol. 302; 1977 Dec 9.
  7th, ed. by Bergmann, P.G. et al. Vol. 262; 1975 Oct 15.

Tran Thanh Van, J. *The standard model and the Supernova 1987A* (XXIInd Recontre de Moriond, March 1987). Gif sur Yvette Cedex, France: Editions Frontieres; 1988.
  Part X is "The Supernova SN 1987A."

Vangioni-Flam, E. et al. *Advances in nuclear astrophysics* (2nd IAP Workshop, Paris, July 7-11, 1986). Gif sur Yvette Cedex, France:Editions Frontieres; 1986.

Wheeler, J. Craig. *Type I supernovae*: proceedings of the Texas Workshop on . . . , Austin:University of Texas at Austin and McDonald Observatory; 1980.

Book Review Sources

Technical Book Review Index, Choice, Book Review Index, Book List, Reference Services Review, RQ, ARBA, Current Book Review Citations, Nature, Today, and the various subject specific journals.

Journals

(computer search determined)

The most frequently cited journals in the area of supernovae are:

Astronomical Journal.
  Cambridge, MA:American Astronomical Society, vol.1- ;1849- .
Astronomy and Astrophysics.
  Berlin:Springer, vol.1- ;1969- .
Astrophysical Journal.
  Chicago:University of Chicago Press, vol. 1- ;1895- .
Astrophysical Journal. Letters to the Editor.
  (Section of above title.)
Astrophysical Journal. Supplement Series.
  Chicago:University of Chicago Press, vol. 1- ;1954- .
Astrophysics and Space Science.
  Dordrecht:Reidel, vol. 1- ;1965- .
International Astronomical Union (IAU) Circulars.
  Cambridge, MA:Central Bureau for Astronomical Telegrams, no. 1884- ;1965- .
Nature.
  London:Macmillan, vol. 1- ;1869- .
Nuclear Instruments and Methods in Physics Research: A.
  Amsterdam:North-Holland, vol. 1- ;1957- .
Physical Review D.
  New York:American Institute of Physics, Series 3. vol. 1- ; 1970- .
Physics Letters B.
  New York:American Institute of Physics, vol. 24B- ;1967- .
Science.
  Washington:American Association for the Advancement of Science, vol. 1- ;1883- .

Table 1 shows the overall and astronomy and astrophysics rankings, as well as the Impact Factor for ISI-covered journals. Also shown in the far right colums are the number of resulting hits from searching "supernova" (truncated) on Physics Abstracts (PA) and Physics Briefs (PB), covering the literature from 1987 through April 27. The highest ISI rankings are generally given to review

TABLE 1

MOST FREQUENTLY CITED ASTRONOMY JOURNALS

TITLE	ISI Overall Ranking	ISI Astronomy Ranking	ISI Impact Factor	# cites/PA	# cites/PB (1987 - April 27, 1988)
Astrophysical Journal Letters	22	2	11.036	36	40
Astrophysical Journal Supplement	76	4	5.585	1	1
Astrophysical Journal	162	5	3.701	100	94
Astronomical Journal	343	7	2.470	23	22
Astronomy & Astrophysics	466	10	2.084	82	80
Astrophysics and Space Science	500+	22	0.617	10	11

Nature	13	–	48	43
Science	18	–	4	3
Physics Letters B	177	–	19	17
Physical Review D	317	–	9	10
Nuclear Instruments and Methods in Physics Research, Section A	–	–	6	1
IAU Circulars	–	–	212	0

Notes: Impact Factor is "the measure of the frequency with which the 'average article' in a journal has been cited in a particular year"

ISI Figures are from Science Citation Index Journal Citation Reports, 1986, Vol. 19

journals, which for supernova literature are not quite as relevant as are current materials.

Indexes/abstracts

Astronomy and Astrophysics Abstracts. Berlin:Springer; 1982- .
   The leading indexing/abstracting tool in astronomy, only released annually, therefore not a current awareness tool.

Astronomy and Astrophysics Monthly Index. Sierra Madre, CA: Olivetree Associates; 1979- .
   The only pure astronomy current awareness source, with permuted title and author indexes. Only covers the technical literature.

Physics Abstracts (Science Abstracts, Part A). London:Institution of Electrical Engineers; 1910- .
   Covers the fields of geophysics, astronomy and astrophysics. Searchable online.

Physics Briefs. New York:American Institute of Physics; 1979- .
   Covers the fields of geophysics, astronomy and astrophysics with a more European perspective than that of *Physics Abstracts*. Online version includes Astronomy and Astrophysics Abstracts since 1987.

Current Contents (Physical, Chemical and Earth Sciences). Philadelphia:Institute for Scientific Information. Weekly.
   A keyword-subject, author, and table-of-contents current awareness source for selected journals.

Science Citation Index. Philadelphia:Institute for Scientific Information; 1955- .
   A keyword-title and author index, plus unique citation indexing to follow research fronts.

SUMMARY OF COMPUTER SEARCHES: For the most current information search manually Astronomy and Astrophysics Monthly Index or the online Physics Briefs file (available only on STN). For comprehensive coverage consider searching Physics Abstracts in addition. Science Citation Index is limited to keyword title access, without assigned subject headings; but it does provide timely access to those articles containing the important title words.

TABLE 2

Computer Searchable Database Results

Search term = "supernova" (truncated)
Search performed on March 9, 1988

	A. & A.M.I.	Chem Abstr.	Physics Abstr.	Physics Briefs	SCI
citations 1980 - present	N/A	1934	2993	3740	625
citations 1987	543	300	532	435	207
citations 1988	53	15	0	28	20
% non-journal	N/A but significant	8	16	26	21
most current record	3/88	3/88	12/87	3/88	2/88

117

NEW REFERENCE WORKS IN SCIENCE AND TECHNOLOGY

Arleen N. Somerville, Editor

Reviewers for this volume are: Kathleen Kehoe (KMK), Columbia University, New York, NY; Donna Lee (DL), University of Vermont, Burlington, VT; and Ellis Mount (EM), Columbia University, New York, NY.

ENGINEERING AND TECHNOLOGY

Space industry international: markets, companies, statistics, and personnel. Edited by Geoffrey K. C. Pardoe. London: Longman; 1987. (Distributed by Gale) 353p. $155.00. ISBN 0-582-00314-8.

An international directory of companies, government agencies and research organizations involved in some aspect of space science and space technology. Products include antennas, computers, rocket engines, solar cells and similar devices. Arranged by continent, then alphabetically by name of the organizations. Besides the usual address and telephone information, the book lists each organization's products, activities, customer names, staff size, publications and senior staff members. There are three indexes—by organization name, products and personal names. Provides a wealth of information about a major sci-tech area of activity, including much information that would be difficult to locate on one's own. (EM)

HEALTH SCIENCES

American nursing. By Vern L. Bullough, Olga Maranjian Church, and others. New York: Garland; 1988. 358p. $60.00. ISBN 0-8240-8540-X.

> The introduction to this fascinating biographical dictionary of 177 U.S. and Canadian nurses points out that nursing is possibly the only profession which women have dominated politically as well as numerically. The biographies describe each nurse's upbringing, achievements, and contributions to nursing. Entries are followed by a list of the nurse's publications and a bibliography of works about each nurse. Only one of the nurses listed is still alive. Two men are included in the volume. A good choice for nursing, history, and women's studies collections. (DL)

American psychiatric glossary. 6th ed. By Evelyn M. Stone. Washington, DC: American Psychiatric Press; 1988. 217p. $11.00. ISBN 0-88048-288-5.

> The American Psychiatric Association's most recent revision of their *Diagnostic and statistical manual* appeared in 1987. Books published before 1987 will not include the most current psychiatric nomenclature, prompting libraries and health professionals to look for recently published psychiatric dictionaries. This new edition of the *Glossary* contains over 200 new terms or revisions among its approximately 3,000 entries.
>
> The volume also includes tables which list commonly abused drugs, drugs used in psychiatry, legal terms, neurological deficits, psychologic tests, research terms, and schools of psychiatry. Definitions are brief and clear. (DL)

Barron's guide to medical & dental schools. 3d ed. By Saul Wischnitzer. Hauppauge, NY: Barron's Educational Series, Inc.; 1987. 324p. $9.95. ISBN 0-8120-3842-8.

> Unlike other Barron's guides, less than half of this guide is devoted to school profiles. Instead, the guide outlines how to prepare for medical and dental school, how to apply, where to find financial aid, and what to expect in school and after.
>
> Profiles include admissions requirements, brief descriptions of the curriculum, student evaluation procedures, and educational facilities. While this guide contains much information that pre-medical and pre-dental students will want to read, many other sources cover some of the same concerns in greater depth. For example, the *AAMC curriculum directory*, published by the Association of American Medical Colleges, contains more complete descriptions of medical school curricula, and would provide a better basis

for deciding which schools to send applications. Meant for individual purchase and possibly undergraduate and high school libraries. (DL)

Dictionary of health services management. 2d ed. By Thomas C. Timmreck. Owings Mills, MD: Rynd Communications; 1987. 675p. $26.00. ISBN 0-932500-56-0.

Words, phrases, legal cases, and abbreviations that relate to the management of health care are explained. A surprising number of terms unique to the field of health services management appear. Swing beds; payment, unified; HANES; prudent buyer principle; and individual practice plan are just a few of the approximately 1,000 terms covered. Many of these terms can be difficult to find in other sources. When an entry has both a general meaning and a meaning specific to health care, both definitions are given. For example, abeyance is defined as "1. Temporary inactivity," and "2. Supervision of personal property . . . until a proper owner appears." (DL)

Directory of fellowship programs in geriatric medicine. 4th ed. New York: American Geriatrics Society; 1987. 165p. $35.00. No ISBN given.

Until the Accreditation Council for Graduate Medical Education incorporates geriatrics residency programs in their *Directory of residency training programs*, the American Geriatrics Society plans to publish this separate directory of fellowship programs in geriatric medicine. Descriptions for both current and proposed programs in the U.S. and Canada are included. (DL)

The directory of online healthcare databases 1987. Los Altos, CA: Medical Data Exchange; 1987. 48p. $29.00. ISBN not given.

Compared with the entries in Cuadra's *Directory of online databases*, I found the descriptions in this directory to be briefer, but on the whole more accurate. Along with the descriptions of the contents of each database, frequency of updates, and number of records, *The directory of online healthcare databases 1987* also provides the costs of the files. While these costs may not be fully up to date, the information does serve as a basis for comparison. Many of the health care databases in this directory were not listed elsewhere. NLM's MeSH file, for example, does not appear in the Cuadra directory.

The directory begins with a short explanation of database searching, mentioning such topics as the procedure for obtaining a password and Boolean logic. Separate subject and producer/vendor indexes complete the directory. (DL)

Disease prevention/health promotion: the facts. Palo Alto: Bull Publishing; 1988. 341p. $24.95. ISBN 0-915950-89-8.

Compiled by the U.S. Department of Health and Human Services' Office of Disease Prevention and Health Promotion, this publication documents the human and economic advantages of preventive medicine. Topics include smoking, stress, dental health, pregnancy, the elderly, minority groups, selected chronic diseases, and delivery of preventive medicine. The sections contain statistical data, case studies, and trends. An extensive list of references supplements each chapter.

This document was originally developed for speech writers and health care journalists but is appropriate for anyone interested in health policy, whether they be health care providers or laity. (DL)

Encyclopedia of neuroscience. 2 vols. Edited by George Adelman. Boston: Birkhauser; 1987. 308p. $150.00. ISBN 0-8176-3335-9.

The publishers have achieved their goal, to compile a comprehensive, first rate, interdisciplinary encyclopedia of the neurosciences. The intended audience is very broad including the general reader, undergraduate students, librarians and professional neuroscientists. The encyclopedia contains over 700 entries written by subject specialists. These entries cover topics from the following areas of the neurosciences: neurobiology, neurochemistry, neurology and its clinical subfields, neuropsychology, and neuroethology. The entries are arranged alphabetically. Some entries are expanded definitions of 200 words or less, many others are subject reviews that are 2,000 to 3,000 words in length. The work is exhaustively indexed, with name and subject indexes that have extensive cross referencing. Although this is a costly reference set, it would be a fine addition to an academic, special or large public library collection. (KMK)

Information resources in toxicology. 2d ed. By Philip Wexler. New York: Elsevier; 1988. 510p. $85.00. ISBN 0-444-01214-1.

Research, clinical, popular, and legislative works from all divisions of toxicology are discussed in this fully annotated bibliography of books, journals, journal articles, newsletters, abstracts, indexes, and audiovisuals. Wexler explains the regulatory processes in the U.S. and hazardous substances communication requirements. The book lists organizations, schools, laboratories, and poison control centers in the U.S. Subsequent chapters cover similar information from an international standpoint. The fine index reflects the overall quality of this publication. (DL)

Medical care chartbook. 8th ed. By Avedis Donabedian, Solomon J. Axelrod and others. Ann Arbor: Health Administration Press; 1986. 483p. $35.00. ISBN 0-910701-17-2.

A compendium of charts which may be used as visual aids by students and lecturers, this volume covers many branches of health care. For additional information regarding the subject of each graph, the authors direct readers to the sources of the data. Subjects include population characteristics, mortality and morbidity data, health care utilization, costs, health personnel, facilities, quality of care and public and private programs. The authors hope that, with advancing computer technology, they will be able to produce new editions of the *Chartbook* more frequently. (DL)

Medical sciences international who's who. 2 vols. 3d ed. London: Longmans; 1987. Distributed by Gale. $450.00 per set. ISBN 0-582-90116-2.

This 2-volume work presents biographical data on around 8,000 senior medical and biomedical scientists, with more than 90 countries. represented. An effort was made to select outstanding scientists for inclusion in the listing. Besides the usual biographical material each sketch includes major publications and highest position held in societies plus fields of interest. There is a rather unusual index in which under the name of each country there is a listing of subjects, such as microbiology, neoplasia or psychiatry, under which scientists are named. Understandably this results in rather lengthy entries for certain subjects in major countries. Provides thorough coverage for most countries, although the U.S.S.R was represented by only 3 scientists, no doubt due to difficulties of obtaining current biographical data from that area. (EM)

Nursing data review 1986. New York: National League for Nursing; 1987. 222p. $24.95. ISBN 0-88737-357-7.

With the continuing shortage of nurses, the data contained in this publication should be of great interest. Tables cover all levels of nursing education in the U.S., from practical nursing to doctoral programs. Factors which affect the number of nurses include the number and distribution of nursing programs, tuition, the number of men and minority students, and the supply of nursing faculty. (DL)

Occupational injuries and illnesses in the United States by industry. 1985. Washington, DC: U.S. Department of Labor;1987. 81p. $6.75. ISBN not given.

> The incidences of illnesses and injuries in 1984 and 1985 for various industries are arranged by SIC codes. Additional tables outline types of diseases and injuries. The amount of worktime lost and the number of fatalities are also listed. As an example, libraries (SIC code 8230) experienced 8.6 lost workdays for every 100 employees. (DL)

Smoking and health, a national status report. Rockville, MD: U.S. Dept. of Health and Human Services; 1986. 467p. $10.00. No ISBN given.

> This government publication covers some of the efforts being made in the U.S. to reduce the prevalence of tobacco cigarette smoking. Beginning with a statistical summary of cigarette smoking in this country, the report goes on to review state and local legislation affecting the sale and use of cigarettes. National and local programs in smoking cessation, prevention, education, and counseling are described and listed by state. The report concludes with summaries of 683 research projects, active in fiscal years '84 and '85, which were related to tobacco use. (DL)

Socioeconomic characteristics of medical practice 1987. Edited by Martin L. Gonzalez and David W. Emmons. Chicago: American Medical Association; 1987. 154p. $45.00. ISBN 0-89970-228-7.

> The "socioeconomic characteristics" detailed in this series relate to the social environment and economic situation of physicians, not patients. Data was gathered through two surveys. Approximately 4,000 physicians responded to the annual core survey, while 2,800 were involved in the second, supplemental, survey. Tables cover various aspects of physician income, hospital utilization by physician, utilization of physician services, and weeks and hours of practice. The data is presented geographically and by broad medical specialty. (DL)

Standards and scope of hospice nursing practice. Kansas City: American Nurses Association; 1987. 28p. $6.00. No ISBN given.

> The ANA has produced a number of publications outlining standards of nursing practice. This guide describes the standards and scope of hospice nursing practice and, since nursing is central to the operation of hospices, also defines acceptable hospice care in general. As the guide describes each standard, the rationale for that standard is explained, and criteria for measuring achievement of the standard are outlined. A list of references and a bibliography are provided. (DL)

USP DI, advice for the patient. 8th ed. Rockville, MD: United States Pharmacopeial Convention; 1988. 1321p. $35.00. ISBN 0-913595-28-4.

This companion volume to *USP DI, drug information for the health care professional*, takes a different approach. Each drug monograph has been written for the patient to read. Health professionals may photocopy pages and give them to patients with their prescriptions, or patients may seek out this information on their own. This publication has several advantages over package inserts or the *PDR*, in that monographs are written in a consistent style, by authoritative, objective authors, specifically for patients. *USP DI, advice for the patient*, wisely cautions patients to consult with their doctor, nurse, or pharmacist if they have any questions. Both volumes, *Advice for the patient* and *Drug information for the health care professional*, may be purchased for the combined price of $115. (DL)

USP DI: Drug information for the health care professional, A and B. 8th ed. Rockville, MD: United States Pharmacopeial Convention; 1988. 2516p. $95.00. ISBN 0-913595-25-X.

The U.S. Pharmacopeia began establishing standards for drug preparations in 1820. Those standards have expanded to include other aspects of dispensing information as well. Indications, chemistry, pharmacology, precautions, side effects, and what advice to give the patient are reported for each drug. A committee of health professionals drafts the drug monographs which are then reviewed by advisory panels, revised, and published in the *USP DI*. Each new edition incorporates comments generated by monographs in previous editions. Appendices on drug use in obstetrics, dental, geriatric, pediatric, and veterinary practice, and a thorough index completes the publications. Updates appear every two months for each annual edition. (DL)

Veterinary medical school admission requirements in the United States and Canada. By Marcia James Sawyer. Bethesda: Betz Publishing; 1987. 149p. $9.00. ISBN not given.

Descriptions of the 27 U.S. and three Canadian veterinary schools include entrance and residency requirements, curriculum, costs, and application information. Other sections cover programs for minority and disadvantaged students, transfer policies, veterinary organizations, information on standardized tests, and tables detailing enrollment success. (DL)

LIFE SCIENCES

Anthropometric standardization reference manual. Edited by Timothy G. Lohman, Alex F. Roche and Reynaldo Martorell. Champaign, IL: Human Kinetics Books; 1988. 177p. $35.00. ISBN 0-873-22121-4.

This manual is the product of an interdisciplinary project to develop standardized methods for anthropometric measurement and data analysis. The chapters were written by experts and reviewed by a consensus committee. The volume's intended audience includes researchers and students of physical anthropology, epidemiology, medicine, physiology, human nutrition or physical education. The volume has author and subject indexes and includes an appendix listing equipment suppliers. The manual would be useful for health sciences, biology or physical anthropology collections. (KMK)

Dictionary of genetics and cell biology. By Norman Maclean. New York: New York University Press; 1987. 422p. $60.00. ISBN 0-814-75438-4.

This dictionary is meant for use by college students and life sciences researchers. The terms were drawn from plant cell biology, molecular genetics, developmental biology and biotechnology. The entries are lengthy and most include background information on the concepts or processes associated with the term. Synonyms and abbreviations are cross-referenced. The dictionary includes five appendices: (1) common and Latin names of key organisms in cell biology and genetics, (2) chromosome numbers in various species, (3) DNA content of haploid genes, (4) the Greek alphabet, and (5) a classification of living organisms. The volume would be extremely useful in any science library reference collection. (KMK)

Guide to molecular cloning techniques. Edited by Shelby L. Berger and Alan R. Kimmel. Orlando, FL: Academic Press; 1987. 812p. $89.00. (Methods in enzymology; v. 152). ISBN 0-121-8205-03X.

This is a comprehensive laboratory manual compiled for use by molecular biologists. It is also a useful reference tool for biological researchers from other fields, or advanced graduate students, who need to employ specific cloning techniques.

The volume contains overview chapters on basic techniques and requirements for cloning such as equipping the laboratory, selecting clones from libraries and identifying specific clones. In addition, there are articles on commonly met methodological problems in the different facets of the work. Many chapters compare different approaches to the same task, presenting the strengths and weaknesses of each. The articles are heavily cross-referenced to facilitate use. In addition there are three indexes: a process guide, an author index and a subject index. The process guide gives the locations, by chapter number, of the specific methods for which protocols have been provided. This process guide is a wonderful convenience in a laboratory reference manual. In all, this is an indispensable acquisition for biological or medical research collections. (KMK)

International directory of genetic services. 8th ed. Edited by Natalie W. Paul. White Plains, NY: The March of Dimes Birth Defects Foundation; 1986. 57p. $2.00. ISBN not given.

By presenting itself as a directory of genetic *services* this publication would seem to appeal primarily to laypersons who seek genetic counseling. While it is possible to locate such services through the directory, programs in many other areas of medical genetics are also recorded. In fact, the foreword indicates that purpose of the directory is to promote communication among genetics researchers.

Medical genetic units are listed by country, director's last name, and genetics services offered. These services cover 26 subspecialties of human genetics, including infertility evaluation, cancer genetics, hematology, population genetics, twin studies, neuro-psychiatric genetics, and physical anthropology. Researchers involved in medical genetics can contact the directors of the appropriate units to exchange data or other information. A psychiatrist studying the genetics of manic depression may write to neuro-psychiatric genetics units near Amish settlements. An AIDS researcher could communicate with immunogenetics units in Africa. (DL)

Life sciences organizations and agencies directory. Edited by Brigitte T. Darnay and Margaret Labash Young. Detroit, MI: Gale Research Co.; 1988. 864p. $155.00. ISBN 0-810-31826-1.

This new Gale directory includes a broad group of life sciences organizations including: scientific associations, international organizations, research centers, consulting firms, government agencies, libraries, and educational institutions. "Life sciences" is defined here to include biology (except neurobiology), biotechnology, agriculture, ecology and the environmental sciences. There are approximately 7,600 listings; most of them were culled from other Gale directories such as the *Encyclopedia of associations*.

The directory contains 18 chapters organized by institutional type. There is a single index containing the associations' names and keywords. The index supplies reference numbers to the entries in lieu of page numbers. Although the book's price is high, it is an excellent reference source for special or academic life sciences libraries. (KMK)

The lipid handbook. Edited by Frank D. Gunstone, John L. Harwood and Fred B. Padley. London: Chapman and Hall; 1986. 869p. $150.00. ISBN 0-412-24480-2.

The Lipid handbook is a reference source for information on lipids and fatty acids. It will be useful to its intended audience—biochemists, physiologists, physicists and physicians. The handbook is divided into two parts. The first part consists of chapters on the chemical composition of the lipids. These chapters also deal with the physical properties of lipids, metabolism, and lipid assays. There is a chapter on the commercial processing of fats and oils and a chapter on medical and agricultural significance of lipids. The text is well organized and contains extensive tables of data on lipid properties. The remainder of the handbook is a chemical dictionary consisting of the lipid and fatty acid entries from the *Dictionary of organic chemistry*. Access to the material is provided by three indexes—a subject index, a molecular formula index and a compound name index. This is a fine reference source on lipids that would be useful in the life sciences, chemistry, and biomedical libraries. (KMK)

Manipulating the mouse embryo: a laboratory manual. Edited by Brigid Hogan, Frank Constantini and Elizabeth Lacy. Cold Spring Harbor, NY: Cold Spring Harbor Laboratory; 1986. 332p. $60.00. ISBN 0-879-69175-1.

This manual was designed for use by biologists who are unfamiliar with recombinant DNA techniques. It is a "how to" book for developing new strains of trangenic mice. Detailed instructions are provided for setting up and maintaining mouse colonies, the culture and transfer of embryos, the introduction of foreign genetic material into the developing mouse embryos and techniques for visualizing genes and gene productions. The volume is illustrated with sketches, electron micrographs and color photographs. There are three appendices: (1) a schematic drawing for assembling a Nikon or Zeiss based microinjection apparatus, (2) a linkage map of the mouse, and (3) suggested readings. There is also an extensive bibliography and a subject index. This comprehensive work will be useful to researchers and advanced graduate students in genetics, embryology and biotechnology. (KMK)

Smith's sea fishes. Edited by Margaret M. Smith and Phillip C. Heemstra. Berlin: Springer-Verlag; 1986. 1045p. $104.00 ISBN 0-38716-851-6.

Smith's sea fishes is a comprehensive identification guide to the 2,200 species of fishes found in South African waters. This impressive compilation is intended for use by marine biologists, icthyologists and serious anglers. Each species of fish has an entry which includes a sketch, physical description, Latin name, English name, Afrikaans name, habitat and geographic distribution. There are also 144 pages of color photographs and illustrations to aid in identification. Access to the entries is provided by three indexes: a scientific name index, an English name index, and an Afrikaans name index. In addition to the identification guide, the book includes a 41-page bibliography on South African icthyology. This is an impressive work, and it would be useful as a reference source in biology, marine biology, or natural history libraries.

Thesaurus of psychological index terms. 5th ed. Washington, DC: American Psychological Association; 1988. 291p. $65.00. ISBN 0-912704-67-5.

This edition of the *Thesaurus* contains 250 new terms and 100 new see references. The main body lists 6,674 see references and posted terms with their relationships to other terms. The entry for each posted term includes scope notes and an indication of how many articles were indexed under the term in the PsycInfo database as of June, 1987.

The Rotated Alphabetic Section displays terms in alphabetical order by each word in the term. Thus, the term Psychological Stress may be found in two places—under Psychological and under Stress. As a new feature in the fifth edition, see references are also included in the Rotated Alphabetic Section. Appendix C presents a chart of the content classification categories and codes used in PsycInfo.

A necessary tool for all searchers of PsycInfo and *Psychological Abstracts*. (DL)

PHYSICAL SCIENCES

Essays on the history of organic chemistry in the United States, 1875-1955. By Dean Stanley Tarbell and Ann Tracy Tarbell. Nashville: Folio Publishers; 1986. 433p. $19.95. ISBN 0-939454-03-3.

Consists of 26 essays written by the authors, arranged more or less in chronological order from 1875 to 1955. Essays contain many citations to the literature, often several scores of them. Pictures are printed for more than a dozen prominent chemists. Includes two indexes, one for personal names and one for subjects. A welcome addition to the literature on the history of science. (EM)

SCIENCE, GENERAL

Encyclopedia of associations: association periodicals. Vol. 2. Science, medicine and technology. Edited by Denise M. Allard and Robert C. Thomas. Detroit: Gale; 1987. 989p. $60.00. ISBN 0-8103-2062-2.

> A new reference work, supplementing the well known *Encyclopedia of associations*. This volume is devoted to sci-tech publications, which include periodicals, newsletters, and proceedings, along with certain publications which revise information previously published, such as yearbooks and handbooks. More than 2,700 titles are listed, with entries listed under such subjects as acoustics, oncology or pediatrics. Data for each entry include title, issuing body, description, editor(s), frequency, price, circulation, and where indexed. There are two indexes, one arranged by the name of the organization and the other by titles and keywords (taken from the titles). There will be two other volumes in the set, one for business/finance and one for social sciences/humanities. A welcome addition to the previously published sets on association data. (EM)

Encyclopedia of information systems and services. 3 vols. 8th ed. Edited by Amy Lucas and Annette Novallo. Detroit: Gale Research; 1988. $400.00. ISBN 0-8103-2532-2.

> An impressive directory to approximately 4,100 organizations, services and systems involved in the production and distribution of information in electronic form. Includes publishers, database products, CD-ROM producers, library management systems, document delivery companies, consultants and professional organizations, to name some of its contents. Volume 1 deals with organizations in the United States, volume 2 is devoted to foreign and international organizations, and volume 3 contains 8 indexes (a listing by organizational name or services, database files, titles of publications, software index, services offered (such as indexing, optical publishing, electronic mail), personal names, geographical location, and subjects of interest. Typical entries supplement customary directory data with descriptions of services and publications, type of clientele, staff size and person to contact for more information. An outstanding compilation. (EM)

Pacific research centres: a directory of organizations in science, technology, agriculture, and medicine. 2d ed. London: Longman Group; 1988. 517p. (Dist. by Gale) $300.00. ISBN 0-582-01608-8.

Provides information about some 3,500 organizations devoted to research located in 21 countries in the Pacific area, such as Australia, China, Hong Kong, Philippines, Taiwan, Thailand and Vietnam. Entries are arranged by countries, in alphabetical order under the country name. Typical entries include name of the organization, address, director, names of departments or laboratories, size of research staff, annual budget for research, areas of research and titles of publications. There are two indexes, one by titles of organizations and the other by subjects of research topics underway. The latter index ranges from aerial photography to frozen foods to zirconium compounds. Should be a great aid to those desiring information about research in this area of the world. (EM)

SCI-TECH IN REVIEW

Karla Pearce, Editor
Giuliana Lavendel, Associate Editor

SEARCH — ONLINE OR MANUALLY?

Anderson, Charles R. Budgeting for reference services in an on-line age. *The Reference Librarian.* 19: 179-194; 1987.

Often online services are difficult to justify in small- to medium-sized libraries. This may be because there has been no attempt to understand the per use costs of print sources. Using *Output Measures for Public Libraries* (American Library Association, 1982) the author offers formulas and guidelines for pricing individual uses of standard reference sources. Cost-effectiveness of online vs. print searching is also discussed. Although this is based on reference service in a small public library in Northbrook, Illinois, the questions asked and alternatives suggested are useful to anyone who is attempting to budget reference services. (KJP)

WAREHOUSE OF THE FUTURE

Williamson, R. The knowledge warehouse: legal and commercial issues. *The Electronic Librarian.* 6(1): 10-17; 1988 February.

The British Library, the Department of Trade and Industry, and Publishers Databases Limited, all in Great Britain, have launched a project to establish a national archive of the electronic form of knowledge works. Most published information passes through this electronic stage; present practice of destroying the electronic form seems wasteful since information in this form might be part of an effort to provide modern, computerized information retrieval. In a year-long project, the legal, including copyright, procedural, and commercial aspects of making pre-published, electronic information available were identified and tested. Through publicity and active exploitation, the trustees of the Knowledge Warehouse hope to bring in more sources and make it more widely known and accessible. This is an exciting idea that many would like to see developed in the U.S. (KJP)

STANDARDS FOR DIGITAL DATA

Buckingham, Michael. The knowledge warehouse: technical issues. *The Electronic Librarian*. 6(1): 6-9; 1988 February.

In a continuation of the previous article, the technical side of text transfer operations are discussed. The components of text—intellectual content, physical and intellectual format and the physical layout—are defined. Problems and advantages of various input formats, e.g., magnetic tape, floppy disk and telecommunications, are discussed. Building on the present nucleus of good practice, the author argues for generic encoding practices and standards for text processing by computer. They not only make sense for the Knowledge Warehouse project but for the future of electronic publishing. (KJP)

INFORMATION GRAZING

Cove, J.F.; Walsh, B.C. Online text retrieval via browsing. *Information Processing and Management*. 24(1): 31-38; 1988.

EYEBROWS is described. It is a prototype software system whose object is to enhance the human information seeking behavior of browsing, which is defined as a search where criteria are vague and the seeker may not know what s/he wants until s/he finds it. The authors divide browsing operations into the components of structure, navigation and semantics. This software is designed to provide the searcher with an overview of the document, opportunities for word association, and the ability to narrow or widen the search as well as to backtrack. The overview and word association functions also send the user on new trails through the browsed text. As a prototype system, EYEBROWS is just a start, but it addresses the important problem of retrieving information in an associative style which is preferred by more than one of us. (KJP)

RISING JOURNAL PRICES

Editors of the *Journal of Academic Librarianship*. Paying the piper: ARL libraries respond to skyrocketing journal subscription prices. *Journal of Academic Librarianship*. 14(1): 4-9; 1988 March.

In a recent questionnaire, JAL questioned directors of ARL libraries about rising journal prices. They asked (1) Is this a serious problem for your library this year? (2) Do you anticipate cutbacks in serials subscriptions this coming year? and (3) If so, how large a percentage? Typically, libraries are cutting back in the range of eight to twelve percent; duplicates are their main targets; monographic acquisitions are being cut as well; some special budgetary allocations from university administrations have been received; despite feeling that journal publishers are mainly responsible for their problems, respondent libraries have not yet adopted any specific policies aimed at publishers; librarians are making special efforts to involve campus officials and faculty in the serials problem; and they are "expanding or intensifying cooperative resource sharing arrangements." Interesting quotes illustrate the frustration experienced by librarians who are heavily dependent on serial publications. (KJP)

THE DIRECTOR MEETS THE PUBLIC

Russell, Ralph E. In search of insight: library administrators work the reference desk. *The Reference Librarian*. 19: 309-314; 1987.

How can administrators find out what their users want, how well they are being served, and how that service can be improved? The author, who is university librarian at Georgia State University, Atlanta, suggests that much can be learned by placing oneself closest to the user—at the reference desk. He found it was healthy to have to defend library policies and procedures to users, and that he became quickly sensitized to areas about which users complained (in this case, the arrangement of the periodicals collection). He also became quite aware of the need for better graphics and signs. In addition, the experience gave him the opportunity to observe and learn from reference librarians, and to demonstrate to faculty and other administrators the importance of librarianship, as opposed to management. He is not bashful to note, however, that as the most highly paid and least skilled reference librarian at the desk, he must occasionally admit to ignorance, and his few hours per week will not enable the reference staff to work fewer hours. A strong case is made for library administrators to leave their offices and meet their users. (KJP)

TIME TO SHIFT THE COLLECTION—AGAIN

Seiler, Susan L.; Robar, Terri J. Reference service vs. work crews: meeting the needs of both during a collection shift. *The Reference Librarian*. 19: 327-340; 1987.

At the Richter Library of the University of Miami, the 7,276 volumes of abstracts and indexes were re-cataloged, re-grouped by subject and shifted. The authors describe in great detail the planning and procedures used for this shift. Seven different factors were included in their formula for gauging how much space would be needed. Shelves and titles were labelled so specifically that the crews could work independently without any extra holding space for "displaced" volumes and without disturbing reference activities. There is a need for reports such as this on an activity that is all too common in science and technology libraries. (KJP)

SCHOLARLY JOURNALS

Basch, N. Bernard. The scholarly journal and the library market. *Scholarly Publishing.* 19(3): 157-162; 1988 April.

America's 33,000 libraries spent $3.7 billion last year for materials; a growing percentage of this budget is dedicated to journal subscriptions. Scholarly publishers at times fail to recognize that there are seven different library segments: academic and research, school, public, medical, law, business, and government libraries. Some special libraries do not fit within these categories, e.g., museum and trade association libraries. All suffer from budgetary problems, exacerbated by subscription cost increases and new title proliferation. Librarians, beleaguered by paperwork, have turned to automated control systems, including those developed by subscription agencies. A discussion on acquisition patterns in the diverse library segments follows. The final section covers marketing techniques for publishers, including the importance of customer service and the impact of volatile currency exchanges. (GAL)

SCIENCE LIBRARIES AND THE FUTURE

Dionne, Richard J. Science libraries at a crossroads. *American Scientist.* 76(3): 268-272; 1988 May-June.

Applications of new technology are of great concern to librarians whose environment is also affected by the rising cost of journals: 1987 subscription prices for European scientific journals rose from 20 to 35%, and 1988 increases are not far behind. While automation is a positive force for developing better user services, costs are a negative factor. Scientists should be aware that such issues will directly impact the future of science libraries in the 21st century. The author, whose experience covers the management of collections at Yale and Syracuse Universities, finds that his observations apply also to libraries abroad and to corporate libraries, which are more sensitive than their academic sisters to economic conditions. Collection development and the selection process are described; book expenditures range from 10 to 15% of the journal budget, which is burdened by new journals coming to join the approximately 50,000 science and technology titles in existence. Focus is on customer service in the high tech, integrated library. Of 50,000 passwords issued for online searching, 20,000 are for end users; this phenomenon will grow, as will the prevalence of CD-ROMs, which brings a whole set of new problems for librarians to consider.

CD-ROM MARCHES ON

Edwards, John. CD-ROM threatens on-line database services. *MacWeek*. 2(22): 40; 1988 May 31.

Why buy knowledge from a single source when another vendor can supply the same information package at a lower price? The database field was soaring a short time ago, but the writing is on the wall. The optical disk, handling upward of 550 Mbytes of memory, is killing online databases, with their slow transmission speeds, high connect charges, and archaic search software. Lockheed Corporation hired a Wall Street firm to investigate DIALOG's sale, and set the price at $200 million; it may be an empty husk, however, since, like most online database providers, DIALOG is only a conduit. The CD-ROM industry still has three problems to solve: cost, lack of product, and incompatibility. Drive prices will fall when production becomes higher, but the industry must adopt a single standard to be successful. There are now two, the High Sierra and Apple's HFS format. Apple is supposed to release High Sierra drives soon, thus unifying the field and hastening the switch from online services to CD-ROMS.

INFORMATION DELIVERY

Brower, Emily. Information at your fingertips. *MacWeek*. 42-44; 1988 April 5.

A landmark decision was handed down last March, allowing regional Bell telephone companies to transmit electronic data. For users of bibliographic databases online, however, the information age has already dawned. The database industry has vendor/producer dichotomy. DIALOG is vendor only, while Knight-Ridder of VU/

TEXT (regional focus) and Mead Data of NEXIS (global view) are also producers, besides being full-text oriented. Vendors offer common search language, but a good way of controlling costs is to use integrated search software. Macintosh developers have not caught up with the PC world in this category; however, Personal Bibliographic Software is working on porting its successful Pro-Search to the Mac, and has already ported Pro-Cite, a database builder. A HyperCard front end for searching DIALOG has been developed with help from Apple, but DIALOG may develop its own Mac product. Desktop Express has been developed by Apple, MCI and Dow Jones.

GROUP INFORMATION PROCESSING

Corcoran, Elizabeth. Groupware. *Scientific American.* 258(7): 110-112; 1988 July.

We are witnessing the emergence of collaboration technology or groupware as a driving force in information processing. Through personal computing, groups of users achieve power over information technology, boosting efficiency four ways: (a) by facilitating joint projects, such as co-authored papers; (b) by disseminating information, such as design changes; (c) by linking people who might otherwise not communicate, and thus germinating new ideas; (d) by capturing discussions and creating a design history helpful for product issues. Workers at universities (M.I.T., Stanford) and corporations (General Motors, Lotus, Xerox PARC) are building "groupware" tools which run on personal computers linked by networks, and are used by researchers and engineers. Collaboration technologies allow one to capture how decisions are made and may offer a learning curve accelerator for competitive purposes.

SCI-TECH ONLINE

Ellen Nagle, Editor

NINTH NATIONAL ONLINE MEETING

The 1988 National Online Meeting, held in May in New York City, featured 76 technical papers, product reviews, exhibits, and a wide variety of satellite events. More than 120 exhibits and 90 product reviews provided conference-goers with information on the spectrum of online and optical databases and services. A new feature this year, the CD-ROM Gallery, offered exhibits and demonstrations of optical products from database publishers, hardware vendors, and CD-ROM distributors. Several technical sessions continued the trend from last year, with presentations about CD-ROM technology. A new topic was introduced this year: hypertext, specifically as related to online searching.

In her introductory summary of the online field, Program Chairman Martha Williams highlighted usage and revenues during the fourth quarter of 1986. During the quarter, 517 databases from 270 producers were used for a total of 689,000 connect hours. Eighty-five and one-half million dollars in revenues were generated during that time. A small number of the 14 vendors of these databases exceeded $10 million in revenues for the quarter. The two highest use vendors were Mead and DIALOG, together accounting for 72% of the usage market and 82% of the revenues. The next five vendors, BRS, STN, West, NLM, and SDC received 25% of the use and 15% of the revenues.

DATABASE NEWS

PTS Newsletter Database Announced

DIALOG searchers now have full-text access to articles from a broad range of specialized industry newsletters. Predicasts' new *PTS Newsletter Database* covers approximately 100 newsletter titles, containing important information about company developments, ventures and activities; new products and applied technologies; market and industry trends and conditions; and government policies, funding, regulation, and legislation.

Sources for the new file include such varied newsletters as the following: *Air/Water Pollution Report*; *APS Review: Oil Market Trends*; *Communications Daily*; *Defense Daily*; *Inside R&D*; *Superfund*. Users can retrieve information from more than 18 industries and international regional areas. The scope of the database includes telecommunications, defense and aerospace, energy, broadcasting and publishing, computers and electronics, environment, and biotechnology. Key areas in which additional newsletter titles are being added include advanced materials, financial services, health care delivery, research and development, and manufacturing automation. The database is international in scope with initial geographic emphasis on such important regions as Japan and the Middle East, in addition to North America and Europe. Records are searchable by industry, title, publisher, and publication date in addition to the complete text.

PTS Newsletter Database has more than 15,000 full-text records, with newsletter title coverage dating back to January 1988. Weekly updates add 1,000 records. The price for searching File 636 is $1.60 per minute. Prints charges are $.60 per full record printed online; $.90 for each offline record.

Chemical Engineering Abstracts Online

The Royal Society of Chemistry has mounted *Chemical Engineering Abstracts* on DIALOG. The database covers all aspects of chemical process engineering, including production plant and pilot scale studies, theory, laboratory experiments, computer applications, relevant physical and chemical property data, plant and personal safety, and environmental issues. The file, which is the online equivalent of the printed source of the same name, extends back to 1971. Records are obtained from 240 regularly scanned core journals, as well as from books, technical reports, and press releases. All records have searchable abstracts; quantitative results are cited wherever possible. Controlled vocabulary indexing terms are used, and broader section headings are assigned to facilitate searching.

Chemical Engineering Abstracts began with approximately 82,000 records. Monthly updates add approximately 500 records. The price for searching File 315 is $1.63 per minute. Each full record costs $.70 online; the offline printing rate is $.35 per record.

BRS Adds New Government Document Databases

Federal Register Abstracts and *Congressional Record Abstracts* are now available on BRS. Online counterparts to the hard copy *Federal Register* and *Congressional Record*, these databases offer information on a wide variety of science and technology subjects.

The *Federal Register* database contains more than 50,000 records, dating from January 1986 to the present. It provides complete coverage of federal administrative and regulatory actions appearing in the publication, which serves as the daily printed record of all government pronouncements. Included are: new rulings, proposed regulations, notices, meetings, hearings, presidential proclamations, determinations and executive orders, public law notices, and notices of rulings taking effect. Each record includes a concise abstract, as well as information on the publication date, type of document, agency or other source of the proposal or ruling, controlled vocabulary terms, and other descriptors. Approximately 700 new and revised documents are added each week.

Congressional Records Abstracts contains more than 100,000 records from the official daily journal of the U.S. Congress. Concise records and abstracts are provided for bills and resolutions and their amendments, committee and subcommittee reports, public laws, schedules of committees and floor actions, executive communications, and speeches, debates and all materials inserted by members of Congress. The database is updated weekly with 1,000 new records.

Both databases are produced by the National Standards Association of Bethesda, Maryland. Each file has a royalty charge for searching of $45. Printed records cost $.30 online and $.25 offline.

SEARCH SYSTEM NEWS

BIOSIS Connection Introduced

BIOSIS has announced a new online system, the *BIOSIS Connection*, featuring an array of low-cost databases. Launched by BIOSIS in May 1988, the *BIOSIS Connection* is designed to support information and communication needs of the research community. Six databases are currently available on the system: *BioExpress, BioBooks, BioMeetings, BioPatents, Serial Sources for the BIOSIS Data Base,* and *Forthcoming Events*. These databases provide access to information from a wide range of sources including journals, books, national and international meetings and U.S. patents. Announcements of upcoming seminars and meetings are also provided online.

The new information system offers two search modes, a Menu Mode designed for the novice searcher, and an Expert Mode for the more sophisticated user. Two subscription plans are also available. Users can choose between a Package Subscription Plan and a Regular Subscription. The Package Plan costs $50 and entitles users to $100 worth of connect time (including hit charges) and a search guide. Those who elect the Regular Subscription are billed monthly for connect time ($35/hour for Menu Mode; $45/hour for Expert Mode). Hits are billed at $.15 each. Telecommunications charges, any special service surcharges, and document delivery are billed separately with both plans.

The *BIOSIS Connection* is available through Tymnet Communications, 7:00 a.m. to 1:00 p.m. Eastern Time, Monday through Friday, and 9:00 a.m. to 1:00 a.m. Saturday. According to BIOSIS, the system can be accessed with any modem-equipped personal computer or terminal device. For more information, or to request a sign-up kit, contact the BIOSIS Marketing Section at 1-800-523-4806.

PUBLICATIONS AND SEARCH AIDS

User-Aid Manual for Agrochemicals

The Royal Society of Chemistry has published the *RSC Agrochemical Services User-Aid Manual*. This manual is designed for searchers of *The Agrochemicals Handbook*, File 306 on DIALOG. The publication includes a detailed description of the contents of the file, controlled vocabulary terms (e.g., company names, agricultural terms), search hints, and sample searches. The manual is available for $27 from the Royal Society of Chemistry, Sales & Promotion Department, The University, Nottingham NG72RD, England.

New Edition of Source Journals in Metals and Materials

Materials Information, the joint information service of ASM International and the Institute of Metals, is offering an updated edition of *Source Journals in Metals and Materials*. Materials Information produces *METADEX, World Aluminum Abstracts, Materials Business File*, and *Engineered Materials Abstracts*. Their new journal guide gives title, standard abbreviation, name and address of publisher, and frequency of publication for over 1,800 technical journals which deal with steels, nonferrous metals, polymers, ceramics, or composite metals. A separate table lists journals according to their field of emphasis. This fourth edition contains about 200 more titles than the previous edition, published in 1986. *Source Journals* can be ordered for $55. Contact: Ms. Debbie Barthelmes, Materials Information, ASM International, Metals Park, OH 44073. Telephone: 216-338-5151, ext. 532.

Nursing & Allied Health Thesaurus Greatly Enhanced

CINAHL, the producer of the *Nursing & Allied Health* database, is offering a revised thesaurus. More than 1,000 new terms have been added to the 1988 *Subject Heading List*, including over 600 new generic drug terms. Cross references from drug trade names to generic names have been added for the first time. The section with research terminology has been reorganized and greatly expanded to enhance retrieval of research and theory articles. Many new nursing and allied health terms have been included, as well as added terms in the fields of psychology, sociology, business, medicine, and education. The 1988 *Subject Heading List* also contains an updated guide to searching the database. The publication is available for $35 from CINAHL, 1509 Wilson Terrace, Glendale, CA 91209-0871. Telephone: 818-409-8005.

For Product Safety Concerns and Information please contact our EU
representative GPSR@taylorandfrancis.com
Taylor & Francis Verlag GmbH, Kaufingerstraße 24, 80331 München, Germany

www.ingramcontent.com/pod-product-compliance
Lightning Source LLC
Chambersburg PA
CBHW052129300426
44116CB00010B/1828